95
Theses
on
Politics,
Culture,
and
Method

95

Theses
on
Politics,
Culture,
and
Method

ANNE NORTON

Yale University Press
New Haven and London

Designed by Judith F. Karbowski-Hall.

Set in Scala Sans and Sabon type by Integrated Publishing Solutions.

Printed in the United States of America by Vail-Ballou Press.

ISBN: 0-300-10011-6 (cloth: alk. paper)

A catalogue record for this book is available from the Library of Congress
and the British Library.

The paper in this book meets the guidelines for permanence and durability
of the Committee on Production Guidelines for Book Longevity of the
Council on Library Resources.

10 9 8 7 6 5 4 3 2 1

Contents

95 Theses on Politics, Culture, and Method   vii

Commentary   1

Afterword   139

95 Theses on Politics, Culture, and Method

1. Culture is a matrix.   1
2. Culture is not a variable.   2
3. Politics is in culture.   7
4. Culture is political.   9
5. Culture is in language.   12
6. Language is political.   13
7. There is no neutral language.   15
8. We are in language.   16
9. Authority is political and literary.   17
10. Culture can be considered as a text.   22
11. Literary devices have direct counterparts in political strategies.   23
12. Culture constitutes the body and makes it readable.   26
13. Gender, race, and sexuality are cultural constructs.   27
14. Commodities serve as semiotic lexicons.   31
15. The natural is a cultural category.   33
16. Culture is an observable concept.   34
17. Culture is made in practice.   36
18. Culture, as practice, is continually changing.   37
19. The formal is always accompanied by an informal counterpart, the structural by the antistructural and the unstructured.   39
20. Change comes from the liminal.   41
21. All cultures are syncretic.   42
22. All cultures are exceptional. No culture is exceptional.   44
23. Culture is wild and various.   45

24. Subjects have multiple identities.   47
25. Identities are performed.   49
26. Identities have multiple expressions.   51
27. Every identity is in reference to a collective.   52
28. Identity and community are coeval.   54
29. Identity and alienation are coeval.   55
30. Every political institution calls for identities.   55
31. Identities make interests. Interests make identities.   57
32. There are no "interests." There are "interests of"
    and "interests as."   58
33. Every identity is partial.   59
34. Community entails alienation.   60
35. Belonging may be expressed as affirmation
    or rebellion.   61
36. Each institution calls for its own resistance.   62
37. There is no culture without resistance.   63
38. There is no culture without internal critique.   65
39. Meaning is made out of difference.   65
40. Power is productive.   67
41. Opposition is productive.   68
42. Lack impels. Lack is productive.   69
43. Power comes from the absence of power.   70
44. The most effective domination is internal.   71
45. The most effective rule is invisible and appears
    as inevitable.   73
46. Domination is through and of the senses.   74
47. Prohibitions produce institutions and resistances.
    Prohibitions interpellate identities.   76
48. Ruling structures constrain the rulers as well as the
    ruled, the advantaged as well as the disadvantaged.   77
49. That which is overcome, remains.   78
50. Nothing runs ahead of its time. Many things run
    ahead of their time.   79

51. Facts do not speak for themselves.   80
52. Facts are made.   80
53. Facts are artifacts of the methods that produce them.   81
54. There are no neutral methods.   82
55. There are no neutral scientists.   83
56. Work speaks simultaneously of its ostensible object
    and of its author and context.   84
57. There are no general laws.   86
58. There is no evidence. Evidence is always of and for
    something.   87
59. Nothing is noncontributory.   88
60. That which is omitted, absent, and silent is as
    important as that which is committed, present,
    and conspicuous.   89
61. Description entails analysis.   90
62. No account can be comprehensive.   91
63. Representation alters the represented.   93
64. Quantification is distortion.   95
65. Formality obscures more than it clarifies.   98
66. Every method has an evaluative hierarchy.   98
67. Every method has an aesthetic.   99
68. Parsimony is an aesthetic criterion.   101
69. The form in which something is expressed determines
    its meaning. The signifier constitutes the meaning
    of the sign.   102
70. Surfaces are as meaningful as that which lies
    beneath them.   103
71. Names constitute. Categories constitute.   104
72. All categories are subject to an interior articulation
    and to an articulation of their relations with others.
    No category is internally homogenous,
    or independent.   106
73. Correlation does not establish causality.   107

74. Accurate prediction is not proof of correct reasoning. 107

75. Replication is not proof. 108

76. Repetitions alter what they repeat. 109

77. Falsifiability does not establish validity. Falsifiability is not a necessary attribute of a theory, nor an index of superiority. 110

78. Subjective satisfaction is not an index of the truth or the merit of a theory. 111

79. Systems of knowledge are systems of power. 113

80. Truth is a cultural category. Truth is in culture. 115

81. Experience confers only a limited understanding. 116

82. Lies and errors are meaningful. 117

83. Time is an attribute of the observer, not of the observed. 119

84. A statement of a causal relation is not a theory. Theory does not require causality. 122

85. Schemes of causality are narrative fictions driven by illusory personifications. 123

86. Culture has dimensions in time and space. 126

87. Cultures have tempi. 127

88. If one can ask where, then one can also ask when. If one can ask when, one can ask where. 129

89. What comes before may have come after. 129

90. The past is accessible only in and as the present. 131

91. The designation of origins is a political act. 133

92. There is no incorruptible discourse. There is no perfect method. 134

93. The ideal appears in the material. 135

94. The abstract appears in the particular. 136

95. Theory cannot exhaust the particular. 137

1. Culture is a matrix.

The old thesis "culture is a network of meaning" gave direction and safe passage to generations of students of culture working in the often hostile environs of the social sciences. It suggested that they might find methodological guidance outside their disciplines, in other social sciences and in literary theory, history, philosophy, and the arts.[1]

The definition can, however, be misleading. It has tempted some to limit culture to meaning alone. Those who use it in this way find themselves looking at a culture made spectral: a culture that lacks materiality. Objects are within the culture only as signs. Understanding culture as meaning alone conceals the linkages between discourse and policy, between semiotics and material conditions. Artifacts, events, practices, and institutions are then placed outside culture, reified, and implicitly constructed as outside and autonomous in relation to the discourses and forces that animate the political.

The virtue of this definition lies in the construction of culture as a matrix. No meaning has a simple, isolated autonomy. Meaning is

1. This thesis was variously attributed, in popular discourse, to Max Weber and Clifford Geertz. Max Weber is a figure of undisputed authority in the social sciences, and offered license and example to many who refused the limits of their disciplines and turned to culture as terrain out of bounds. *The Methodology of the Social Sciences* (trans. and ed. Edward Shils and Henry Finch [New York: Free Press, 1949]), perhaps because it is not as widely read as other works, continues to offer a devastating critique of common practices in the social sciences. Geertz, Marshall Sahlins, and other anthropologists were also enormously important in justifying culture to political scientists. "The Balinese Cockfight" and Negara were less important in this respect than *The Interpretation of Cultures* (New York: Basic Books, 1973) and *Local Knowledge* (New York: Basic Books, 1983). Marshall Sahlins's *Culture in Practice* (New York: Zone Books, 2000), *Islands of History* (Chicago: University of Chicago Press, 1985), and *Culture and Practical Reason* (Chicago: University of Chicago Press, 1976) gave an example of studies fusing the concerns of space, time, and power that preoccupy work far from the heartland of anthropology.

something to be triangulated, a set of relations to be determined, always inflected by the angle of approach. No element of culture, no person, no event, no artifact, can be isolated from this network without impairing our ability to see its significance. The proliferation of relations through which and in which a subject, artifact, or event is seen not only expands one's understanding of the object, it also renders it more exact, more refined, more precise, and more rigorous. One of the powerful and powerfully useful effects of this recognition is to diminish the standing of parsimony as an evaluative criterion.

Another virtue of the idea of culture as a network of meaning lay in the ambiguous meaning of network, and the oblique suggestion that meaning grows out of and finds its meaning within networks—that meaning belongs to the common. Meaning is a common possession, held in common: between people who gesture, speak, and write, who share a common language and common sense. Meaning is common in another sense: because it belongs to the ordinary, to the everyday.

The idea of culture as a matrix directs us to look at culture not only as a field or as a network but also as a medium—the medium in which we are cultured. Yet if meaning is a field and a whole, it is also that which lies between: the interval between one person and another, between one person and the surrounding world.

2. Culture is not a variable.

Culture is not a "dependent" or "independent" variable. Culture is not a variable at all. The practice of taking culture as a variable, occasionally offered as an exhortation to methodological rigor, is the work of ignorance.

Culture is commonly employed as a variable in two ways. In the first, some institution, practice, or other feature is studied in two or more cultures. Differences are then ascribed to "culture." In this approach, each culture is regarded as distinct and monolithic. Differences, particularly the constitutive oppositions that figure in the construction, practices, and discourses of particular cultures, are erased or elided. The syncretic character of cultures is similarly erased or elided. The difference between the cultures is presumed at the outset, concealing points of commonality and reifying a possibly unjustified distinction. Research into points of intersection, exchange, and circulation—trade relations, intellectual exchanges, the transmission of practices and texts, the borrowing of institutions and rituals—is foreclosed. Knowing that "Islam" is different from "the West," we are impelled to ask Why? Likenesses—in institutions, systems of knowledge, understandings of virtue, or economic practices—cannot answer that question. Differences within a culture are likewise denied at the outset, for acceptance of the question obliges us to assume the unity and cultural integrity of France and Germany, Lima (Peru) and Lima (Indiana) in the West; Morocco, Cairo, Indonesia, and Pakistan in Islam.

The second means of employing culture as a variable takes "culture" as an analytic category comparable to "institutions," "class," or "nature." This approach covertly contends that institutions, or laws, or economic practices are somehow distinct from culture. We might be told, for example, that it is "legal apartheid . . .—not 'cultural' factors like religion or the legacy of colonialism—that explains why some people thrive and others don't."[2] Both law and a distinctive set of legal practices—"legal apartheid"—are placed outside culture. Religion and "the legacy of colonialism" are within it. This is nonsense. The laws and legal practices described are related intellectually and historically to both religion and the legacy of colonialism. More importantly, legal systems—all legal systems, no less than the distinctive set of legal practices described in the article—are fully within cultures. Lawyers and judges, legislators and executives, the police, petitioners, defendants, prosecutors, bu-

2. Matthew Miller, "The Poor Man's Capitalist" in *The New York Times Magazine,* July 1, 2001, 44. Miller ascribes this view to Hernando de Soto. The error in the understanding of culture is his, however, not de Soto's.

reaucrats, and regulators are within their cultures. The systems of reasoning they apply are within cultures. Practices employed to en-force—or evade—the law evolve within networks of other cultural practices. The discourses of law and lawlessness are within cultures. So it is with institutions. Those who staff institutions bring the lan-guages, social practices, and norms of their cultures with them. The buildings that house institutions are built according to particular cultural norms and aesthetics. The idea of the institution is embed-ded within particular cultural discourses. The categories "class," "nature," and the rest do not exist outside and apart from culture. Applying such categories is perhaps the most common, and cer-tainly the most absurd, method of employing culture as a variable. A variant employs culture as a "residual variable," a category made up of all that is left over after the relevant analytic categories have been employed. For all its absurdity, this method at least tacitly ac-knowledges the inability of any set of variables to furnish material for a comprehensive account and implies, correctly, if inadvertently, that culture is left over, or left out, of the analysis proper.[3]

Both approaches foreclose the possibility of effective research into questions of culture by abridging the inquiry at the outset. Speaking of culture as a variable permits researchers to evade the obligation to specify the question more precisely. Researchers should be obliged to specify what particular features, practices, institutions, discourses, or structures of a given culture are being examined, to study their structures and operation. They should supply not merely an identification of "culture" as the site of variation but also a specific account of the particular mechanisms within or between cultures that are responsible for the variation.

Taking culture as a variable constructs the researcher as a being capable of abstraction from culture. We are required, however, to acknowledge our embeddedness in particular cultures, the embed-dedness of the methods and categories we employ, and the cultural context and significance of the questions we ask.

---

3. The view of culture as a "residual variable" gives it a family resemblance to Lacan's "objet a."

The account given here begs the question What is culture? and the attendant, critically motivated question Is nothing outside culture? The answer to the latter question is: no, there is nothing outside culture for us. Nothing we study is outside culture. The enterprise of studying it would bring it within culture, if it were not already there. There is little that can be plausibly argued to be outside culture in any sense at all. The most commonly contended for classes are material objects, the objects of mathematics, and natural (or human) rights and laws. Foucault and other scholars have effectively demolished the notion that material objects have conceptual integrity outside culture and have reminded us of the telling differences in the perception and classification of these objects in different cultural contexts.[4] Mathematicians readily acknowledge the cultural character of mathematics. Those who contend for the priority of human and natural rights to culture nevertheless recognize themselves as arguing for these in given cultural contexts and for the necessity of establishing these within cultures. Those who contend for the existence of matter, material objects, ideas, or rights outside culture similarly recognize that matter is brought within culture, worked, made into material objects, assaulted, categorized, studied, and exchanged within culture.

The former question What is culture? is a question best evaded. Meaning, as Wittgenstein observed, is made in practice.[5]

The attentive reader will observe that it is the practice of this author to use the word culture as if it had several related, but by no means exactly coincident, meanings. This is both inevitable and deliberate. Words have the capacity to contain these constellations of related meanings, a quality that belongs to language. Those who seek to obtain a single, exact, and unvarying definition for terms in the social (or other) sciences will find themselves engaged in a futile enterprise, for language is made in practice, and meanings are made

4. Michel Foucault, *The Archaelogy of Knowledge* (New York: Pantheon, 1972).

5. Ludwig Wittgenstein, *Philosophical Investigations,* trans. G. E. M. Anscombe (New York: Macmillan, 1968), 195, 197.

in difference. It is more profitable to recognize and exploit the range of meanings offered in the words we use. The effort to divest a concept of its ambiguity distances it from practice. Because practice often outstrips method in theoretical sophistication, methodologists are well advised to avoid efforts at definition. Such efforts make a word a term of art and strip it of the vigor, range, and refinement of a concept at work in the world. Each concept, each idea, each name is capacious enough to comprehend multiple, often contending meanings; each evokes a complex of historical and literary references. The problem of multiple meanings is thus neither finally solvable nor, finally, a problem. These multiple meanings are definitive: they define the field in which meaning is produced and contested, and the variations and contradictions within that field make possible greater precision and refinement in the use of the concept than a necessarily crude reduction could provide.

2a. There are no variables.

Mindful of this critique of the use of culture as a variable, and the language of variables altogether, one might declare that all use of variables should be abandoned. It is not my project to take crutches from the injured. We should reverse the assumption that arguments should be stated, and projects conceived, in terms of their dependent and independent variables, and that projects that do not follow this pattern should be dismissed. The burden of justification should be on those who employ this mode of expression.

Research strategies that employ variables rely on abstracting a particular relation from others to which it is allied in order to clarify, and consequently examine, that single and particular relation. This abstraction hinders research strategies that aim at showing how a particular relation is allied with others and at delineating the systems (structural and discursive) in which it is embedded. The discourse of variables implicitly invests each variable with an abstract, conceptual integrity and autonomy. The use of variables thus tends to diminish, where it does not foreclose, the recognition of causal reciprocities and the imbrication of variables with one another. The clear causal relations that appear to emerge from analyses employing dependent and independent variables are not discoveries made through the clarifying effects of abstraction, they are rhetorical effects of an analytic mode that imposes a fictive linearity. To avoid these deceptive and misleading effects, methods employing variables should be limited to the examination of those phenomena and situations that meet the presupposed conditions. These are very few.

3. Politics is in culture.

This thesis, like many of those I put forward, admits of multiple readings. The most straightforward uses the ordinary language meaning of *politics*, which refers to the processes of the state and governance, and the challenges and resistance to those. Rulers, elections, the institutions of government, bureaucrats, candidates, legislation, laws, boycotts, demonstrations, and coups are all within culture. They occur within specific cultural contexts; they operate within specific cultural limits. They use references, metaphors, symbols, strategies, structures, and discourses that belong to specific cultures. Even charisma, perhaps the most inchoate and anti-institutional of political phenomena, is interpellated, produced, and validated within a particular culture: "it finds its limits within their circle."[6]

Politics in the Knesset is not confined to Israel, however, nor is the meaning of the Diet limited to Japan. Particular political institutions may have a presence in a number of widely varying cultures. Institutional rivals inevitably have a presence in one another's calculations, conceptions of the field, and in each rival's self-definition. The Knesset has a presence in American culture, notably in the de-

---

6. Max Weber, *From Max Weber: Essays in Sociology,* ed. H. H. Gerth and C. Wright Mills (New York: Oxford University Press, 1973), 247.

bates, hopes, calculations, concerns, and identities of American Jews. At certain moments, during attempted American interventions in the peace process, for example, the presence of the Knesset may also be visible (and active) in a broader American cultural discourse. Analysis of the intersections, overlaps, and of course the disjunctions of the cultural contexts in which a given political actor, institution, process, or practice is embedded is an especially important and fecund field for research. Without the double recognition that politics is in culture, and that the particular political institutions, events, subjects, and actors are in not one culture but several, it will be impossible to do this work.

The recognition that political institutions are produced by, and embedded in, a cultural matrix is simple, critical, and pervasively neglected. The recognition that "rational actors" are cultural subjects, possessed of (or by) preferences formed within culture, has become ubiquitous, although it is frequently neglected in practice.[7] The recognition that the instrumental calculations of these rational actors derive from and accord with culturally specific forms of rationality is also well established.[8] The recognition that states, bureaucracies, political institutions, and party and electoral systems are involved in and produced by a cultural matrix would seem to be inevitable and irrefutable. These recognitions act through and upon people who come to them shaped by cultural forces and carrying cultural forces within them. They act through and within languages and more local discourses, peculiar to particular cultures and contexts. Yet many researchers continue to act as if institutions were not merely conceptually, but actually, separable from cultures. The effects of this willful blindness are pervasive in economics and among

7. On the imbrication of preferences in cultures, see Amartya Sen, "Rational Fools," *Philosophy and Public Affairs* 6 (1977): 317–44. For a critique of the neglect of this (and other) principles, see Jon Elster's review of Robert Bates, Margaret Levy, Jean-Laurent Rosenthal, Avner Greif, and Barry Weingast, *Analytic Narratives, American Political Science Review,* September 2000.

8. On the cultural specificity of forms of rationality and systems of calculation, see Michel Foucault, *The Archaeology of Knowledge,* trans. A. M. Sheridan Smith (New York: Pantheon, 1972).

the imitators of economics in political science.[9] Economic practices occur in the most ordinary and pervasive of cultural contexts, inseparable in practice from the cultural matrix in which they are embedded. Yet the discourse of economics too often proceeds as if "economic forces" operated independently, unconstrained by the cultures in which they occur.

This thesis can also be read more broadly as an assertion that culture is penetrated, or even permeated, by politics. Read in this way, it is close to the thesis that follows.

4. Culture is political.

This thesis, like one it follows, can be read with differing intonations. The ordinary language reading affirms the political significance of artifacts and activities relegated to the narrowest meaning of *culture*: graffiti, rap, rai, photography, and television, for example. These and other artifacts and practices once regarded as trivial—or private—are recognized in this thesis as political. This reading was articulated both in the academy and in the street. It has been given force and substance in the work of innumerable scholars, particularly in social history and cultural studies.[10] E. P. Thompson taught

9. For critiques of economics as a cultural practice, see Donald N. McCloskey, *The Rhetoric of Economics* (Madison: University of Wisconsin Press, 1983). Powerful counterexamples, attentive to economics as a constellation of cultural practices, are furnished by recent work in political economy, including Michael Storper and Robert Salais, *Worlds of Production* (Cambridge, Mass.: Harvard University Press, 1997); Hernando de Soto, *The Mystery of Capital* (New York: Basic Books, 2000); Fernando Coronil, *The Magical State* (Chicago: University of Chicago Press, 1997); *Economics & Language,* ed. Willie Henderson, Tony Dudley-Evans, Roger Backhouse (New York: Routledge, 1993); *The Social Life of Things,* ed. Arjun Appadurai (Cambridge: Cambridge University Press, 1986); Arturo Escobar, *Encountering Development* (Princeton, N.J.: Princeton University Press, 1995); Dani Rodrik, *The New Global Economy and Developing Countries* (Washington, D.C.: Overseas Development Council, 1999).

10. This is a vast literature; I can give only a sampling here. Exemplary works in social history include E. P. Thompson, *The Making of the English*

us that class identity, solidarities, allegiances, and enmities were formed and experienced beyond the confines of what had previously been regarded as politics. Eric Hobsbawm saw the politics in forms of banditry previously regarded as mere criminality. This observation opened the way to investigations into the politics of criminality. Social historians not only learned about politics from cultural artifacts and practices, they also saw those artifacts and practices as political. Studies of minstrelsy and blackface by Michael Rogin and Eric Lott showed the role of music and performance in racial politics. Rogin's reading of Cold War films showed the extension of Cold War ideology into popular culture. Kaja Silverman's study of postwar films displayed not only state activity in the effort to return a demobilized military to domesticity but also, and more importantly, the state's reliance on particular familial and sexual regimes.

The political significance of works and acts formerly regarded as outside the realm of politics was brought to the fore historically by political strategies employed in the 1960s and 1970s, and by the American "culture wars" of the last quarter of the twentieth century. Feminists, continually confronting the insistence that such matters as marital rape belonged not to the public and political realm but to the private sphere, recognized that drawing the boundaries of politics was itself a political act: impelled by considerations of power

---

Working Class (London: V. Gollancz, 1963), and *Customs in Common* (New York: New Press, 1991); Eric Hobsbawm, *Bandits* (London: Weidenfeld & Nicolson, 1969); *The Invention of Tradition*, ed. Eric Hobsbawn and Terence Ranger (Cambridge: Cambridge University Press, 1983); Natalie Zemon Davis, *Return of Martin Guerre* (Cambridge, Mass.: Harvard University Press, 1983). Exemplary works in cultural studies include Kwame Anthony Appiah and Henry Louis Gates, Jr., *The Dictionary of Global Culture* (New York: Knopf, 1997); Jodi Dean, *Aliens in America: Conspiracy Cultures from Outerspace to Cyberspace* (Ithaca, N.Y.: Cornell University Press, 1998); Thomas Dumm, *united states* (Ithaca, N.Y.: Cornell University Press, 1994); Carlo Ginzburg, *Night Battles: Witchraft and Agrarian Cults in the 16th and 17th Centuries* (Baltimore: Johns Hopkins University Press, 1983); Peter Manuel, *Cassette Culture: Popular Music and Technology in North India* (Chicago: University of Chicago Press, 1993); Greil Marcus, *Lipstick Traces: A Secret History of the Twentieth*

and identity and having profound effects on these. Protestations that racial and gender differences were the work of nature revealed the political power operating in the dichotomy of nature and culture and opened questions concerning the political effects of such divisions and dichotomies. Conservatives argued that political institutions relied on cultural supports, and that particular social and cultural configurations, notably in the family, were necessary to preferred political arrangements. All came to recognize that politics was present, and political projects (not always consciously conceived) were at work not only in high and popular arts but also in the sciences, technologies, and, perhaps most effectively and dangerously, in common sense.

One can also read this thesis mindful of the concept of the political. In this reading culture appears, as it has in recent American political history, as the theater of the agon, the site of those necessarily participatory public contests that constitute polities. Culture is a fight. This reading of the thesis marks its relation to democratic politics in particular. If politics is understood as concerning the people, then those everyday practices through which and in which people live their ordinary lives call for particular study.

These two theses on politics and culture indicate that the idea of "political culture" is misleading and should be abandoned. This concept, which I used in my earlier work, suggests that "political

---

Century (Cambridge, Mass.: Harvard University Press, 1989); Michael Rogin, *Blackface, White Noise: Jewish Immigrants in the Hollywood Melting Pot* (Berkeley: University of California Press, 1996); Andrew Ross, *No Respect: Intellectuals and Popular Culture* (New York: Routledge, 1989); *Microphone Fiends: Youth Music & Youth Culture*, ed. Andrew Ross and Tricia Rose (New York: Routledge, 1994); Ikuya Sato, *Kamikaze Biker: Parody and Anomy in Affluent Japan* (Chicago: University of Chicago Press, 1991); Emma Tardo, *Clothing Matters: Dress and Identity in India* (Chicago: University of Chicago Press, 1996); Michael Taussig, *The Devil and Commodity Fetishism in South America* (Chapel Hill: University of North Carolina Press, 1980); *The Cultural Studies Reader*, ed. Simon During (New York: Routledge, 1999). The journals *Representation, Public Culture, Critical Inquiry* and *Theory & Event* have served as important sites for this work.

culture" is somehow separable from culture. The concept claims, obliquely, that culture can be free of politics, and politics of culture. This is wrong. I have learned to argue instead for understanding the political as an aspect of culture, and culture as the field in which politics is conceived and enacted.

5. Culture is in language.

Language is the medium of culture. For us, those who are in language, language is not only the means by which things are named but the schema in which things are placed in relation, and the medium in which those names and those relations are changed. Language is, in the idiom of the labs, the medium in which we are cultured: the substance in which we are formed, the environment in which we grow.

This thesis pays homage to Gadamer's revealingly multivocal statement "We are in language."[11] It captures one aspect of what has been called the "linguistic turn" in the social sciences. Several currents fed into this confluence, among them Wittgenstein's inquiries into language, the structuralisms of Saussure and Lévi-Strauss, the methods of Nietzsche and Heidegger, Habermas's work on communication, and the privileged position of language in the work of Lacan, Derrida, Irigaray, and Wittig.[12]

11. Hans-Georg Gadamer, *Philosophical Hermeneutics,* trans. and ed. David Linge (Berkeley: University of California Press, 1976).
12. Ferdinand de Saussure, *Course in General Linguistics,* trans. Roy Harris, ed. Charles Bally and Albert Sèchehaye (London: Duckworth, 1983); Claude Lévi-Strauss, *Triste Tropiques,* trans. John and Doreen Wightman (New York: Penguin 1973); Martin Heidegger, *On the Way to Language,* Jürgen Habermas, *Theory of Communicative Action,* trans. Thomas McCarthy (Boston: Beacon Press, 1984); Jacques Derrida, *Of Grammatology,* trans. Gayatri Chakravorty Spivak (Baltimore: Johns Hopkins University Press, 1976); Jacques Lacan, *Ecrits,* trans. Alan Sheridan (New York: W. W. Norton, 1977); Luce Irigaray, *Speculum of the Other Woman,* trans. Gillian Gill (Ithaca, N.Y.: Cornell University Press, 1985); and Monique Wittig, *The Straight Mind,* trans. Marlene Wildeman (New York: Beacon Press, 1992). For a useful summary, see Kaja Silverman, *The Subject of Semiotics* (Oxford: Oxford University Press, 1983).

One need not swim in this current to accept the thesis. A more conservative reading would simply affirm that language carries culture within it. The words *mate* and *class* carry different meanings in the countries of the English-speaking world. Words and phrases carry references to history and politics, literature and popular culture. The phrase "my fellow Americans" once called up the face and intonations of Lyndon Johnson. This reading could also be rendered by a reversal: language is in culture, enmeshed in a network not only of meanings but also of images and institutions, formulae and practices. Nietzsche's reading of *schuld* [guilt] in *On the Genealogy of Morals* shows how the word *schuld* not only holds within it a set of references but also maps a process of development.[13] One can read in *schuld* not only a meaning (many meanings) and a set of references but also the genealogy of a concept and a particular subject, a being with the right to make promises.

The hazard of this thesis is in the temptation to read it narrowly and argue that culture is not in language, but merely in the literary products—speeches, texts, documents, novels, poetry, pamphlets, etc.—of human beings. Later theses will show the ways in which this errant understanding of language as immaterial and ineffectual has been undermined in the practice and study of politics.

6. Language is political.

Language is a medium of utterance in the strictest and most expansive sense: a means of movement into the external world, a medium in which interiority escapes the self. This process is reciprocal: the self extends its will, its thoughts, itself, into the external world, and the world enters the innermost self through the medium of language.[14]

13. Friedrich Nietzsche, *On the Genealogy of Morals,* trans. Walter Kaufmann and R. J. Hollingdale (New York: Vintage Books, 1989).

14. This thesis is taken from Wittgenstein. Wittgenstein argues that language is necessarily a collective enterprise, "founded on convention" (Wittgenstein, *Philosophical Investigations,* 355). See also 265, 279.

Knowing that language is political, we know that we can look to language—to texts and utterances of all kinds—to see politics at work. Any text, written or spoken, may be dense with references. Historical references may identify a present conflict with an earlier one, and through that identification shape the reader's apprehension of the present conflict. They can be deployed to evoke favorable or unfavorable judgments of individuals or events.

Politics is present in more subtle references as well. Each word has not only a definition but a set of connotations that inflect it. Accordance to certain linguistic conventions makes a text "poetic" or "scientific." Accordance to other conventions enables the informed reader to place the text in a discipline and to triangulate the place of the text in conflicts within that discipline.[15] An informed reader can say with some ease "this is Lacanian psychoanalytic theory" or "this is rational choice." A deft or erudite reader can say "this is influenced by Koolhaas" or "this witticism mocks Montaigne." In looking for politics in language, we can ask questions not only of the content but also of the forms of language. We can ask, for example, what kind of listener a particular speech calls forth and what kind of speaker it implies. We can ask what it means to say "we" in a particular context, or whether the "we" or "he" or "I" of a speech is raced or gendered. We can ask what it means to take something as an object. We can ask how a question limits the responses it invites or how the statement of a problem limits proposals for its resolution. We can listen for irony, we can look for subtexts. We can use exegesis, hermeneutics, deconstruction, and other techniques to elucidate the relations articulated by and within the text. We can ask what is not said. We can ask what cannot be said. We must then bring these inquiries, these techniques, to bear on our own uses of language. Knowing that language is political, we must consider the

15. *The Rhetoric of the Human Sciences: Language and Argument in Scholarship and Public Affairs*, ed. John S. Nelson, Allan Megill, and Donald McCloskey (Madison: University of Wisconsin Press, 1987); Donald McCloskey, *The Rhetoric of Economics* (Madison: University of Wisconsin Press, 1985).

workings of politics in what we read. We cannot pretend to escape politics in what we write.

7. There is no neutral language.

Language belongs to nations, peoples, and communities. Language carries within it references to relations of power. Language interpellates, structures, preserves, and undermines relations of power. Language is not a neutral medium. All research, and all accounts of research, must attend to the ways in which the means of expression inflects that which is expressed. One might read this thesis remembering Karl Marx. Language, in this reading, is the means of production. We produce in it and through it. Power and identities are produced through and in relation to that means of production, and here much more intimately than elsewhere. The I that speaks, the eye that sees, are made in language. They are given to us not as tools but as the hand is given, and we commonly use them unconscious of their effects. One might read the thesis mindful of Barthes, and Barthes's observation that the sign comprises both signified and signifier and that the signifier is not simply the vessel, but the maker, of meaning. The flag is the tattered cloth as well as the nation it symbolizes, the *salibiyun* were made by the *salib* that marked them as well as by scripture, doctrine, and community.[16]

One can strive to eliminate evidence of overt partisanship from one's writing. One can, in an interview or a survey, attempt to avoid questions that elicit particular responses, preclude others, or silence issues. One cannot, however, escape that which speaks in language: that etymology, that history, that present politics, that social order, or those conventions that make a response acceptable or intelligible. Language is full of meanings beyond our reach or control. Those meanings may speak in language or they may remain silent, but their presence makes neutrality impossible.

16. Roland Barthes, *Mythologies,* trans. Annette Lavers (New York: Farrar Strauss Giroux, 1972), 115.

8. We are in language.

We are in language.[17] Our being and presence is in language. We become as we hear, gesture, and cry out. We become as—and what— we read and write. Language, each language, calls a particular subject into being. The one who says "I" becomes the individual.[18] The one who understands herself in "she" and *"unti"* and *"française"* enters femininity and the systems of gender and sexuality.[19] Even that which is often presented as the precondition for language, the speaking, writing body, is interpellated by language. We find ourselves in bodies already named, already conceived for us, with hands and eyes and mouths we are not only to have but to use and understand in certain specific, already conceived ways. We enter a world made for us in language, filled—through language—with meaning, sentiment, and sensation. Words are not simply vessels into which one pours meaning or tools used to transmit internal apprehensions—thoughts, passions, needs, desires, opinions, insights—to another. Words and grammars shape the meaning they convey, and they do more.

One might also say, with Lacan, that it is not we who speak in language but language that speaks in us.[20] When we speak, we speak in and according to the conventions governing language use. Linguistic structures are visible in what we say and how we say it. We speak not only through language but in language. Language serves us, but we are its creatures, and we speak for it, as well as for ourselves.

17. Gadamer, *Philosophic Hermeneutics,* 3–17, 31–32, 35.
18. This recognition extends into popular culture. An episode of *Star Trek: The Next Generation* treats the ability of the Borg Hugh (named because he understood "you" to refer to him) to use "I" of himself as the act that separates him from the collective being of the Borg and makes him an individual.
19. There is an extensive literature on the relation of gender and sexuality to language. I only gesture to that literature here. See Jacques Lacan, *Ecrits,* trans. Alan Sheridan (New York: W. W. Norton 1977), *New French Feminisms,* ed. Elaine Marks and Isabelle de Courtivron (New York: Schocken Books, 1981).
20. Jacques Lacan, "The Mirror Stage," in *Ecrits,* 1–7.

9. Authority is political and literary.

If language is political, politics is linguistic. Consider the double meaning of authority. The author (in the literary sense) exercises authority (in the political sense). This is most visible in those literary documents that are already understood as political acts: constitutions, presidential decrees, *fatwas*. The authors of these works acted politically in their writing. It is, however, not the content of the work but its form that makes writing authoritative in the political sense. Political authority is exercised in novels as well as *fatwas*, in poetry as well as constitutions, in scholarly works as well as presidential decrees.

Consider the orientalists.[21] Their literary work gave them authority not only over the imagined world of the Oriental but also over specific Oriental subjects who would, thereafter, be seen through the categories of orientalism and assigned the qualities proper to the Oriental. Consider the *Requerimento*. This text and others like it not only alluded to violence, they produced it.[22] The work of postcolonial scholars became necessarily indifferent to the boundary between literature and the social sciences. Those who looked at British and French colonialism saw the colonizers attempting, with particular vigor in the French case, to establish political through literary primacy, employing the language of empire as a means of access to authority, a mode of assimilation, and a method for the transmission of values and cultural hierarchies. Scholars also learned to recognize the confluence of political and literary authority from those who wrote in and out of coloniality and postcoloniality. For Leopold Senghor there was no boundary between literature and politics.[23]

21. Edward Said, *Orientalism* (New York: Random House, 1978).

22. Stephen Greenblatt, *Learning to Curse: Essays in Early Modern Culture* (New York: Routledge, 1992), 26–30. See also Tzvetan Todorov, *The Conquest of America* (New York: Harper and Row, 1984).

23. Senghor was the founder of the Negritude movement and president of Senegal from 1960–80. He is the author of *Collected Poetry*, trans. Melvin Dixon (Charlottesville: University Press of Virginia, 1991), *Oeuvres Poetiques*

Nor is such a boundary observed by Assia Djebbar, Nawal as Sa-
dawi, Salman Rushdie, or, for that matter, Ruhollah Khomeini. The
insistence of many social scientists on "value neutrality" and their
allegiance to the ostensibly apolitical methods of statistics and neo-
classical economics drove the study of politics out of political science, sociology, (and to a lesser extent, history and anthropology)
to the disciplines of English and comparative literature. The insistence of other social scientists on studying the workings of power
rather than method, and the research demands of the politics of the
late twentieth century, brought the study of politics back to the social sciences. The demands of history—and politics—have left the
partisans of a social science deaf to the humanities no defense but
the bald assertion "That's not political science."

A more sophisticated defense of the boundary between politics
and literature has been furnished by Jürgen Habermas. Habermas
deprecates the view that "the genre distinction between philosophy
and literature dissolves upon closer examination," which he im-
putes to literary critics and their apostate philosophic patrons Heidegger, Adorno, and Derrida.[24] The construction is a somewhat
disingenuous one, which succeeds in its maintenance of disciplinary
boundaries only through the excommunication of that rather
significant number of philosophic heretics who "use the fragment as
an expository form" and "place any system under suspicion," and
by a conflation of literary criticism and the writing of fiction.[25]
Habermas affirms the "polar tension between world-disclosure and
problem-solving."[26] Habermas's metaphor argues obliquely (and
correctly) that this "polar tension" constructs and orders a world.

(Paris: Editions de Seuil, 1990), and *On African Socialism,* trans. Mercer Cook
(New York: Praeger, 1964).

24. Jürgen Habermas, *The Philosophic Discourse of Modernity,* trans. Fred-
erick Lawrence (Cambridge, Mass.: MIT Press, 1987), 189.

25. Habermas, *Philosophic Discourse,* 187, 199. The apostate philosophers
would include Plato, Montaigne, Montesquieu, Rousseau, Nietzsche, and
Wittgenstein.

26. Habermas, *Philosophic Discourse,* 207.

In that world, problem-solving can proceed without reference to "world disclosure." This was a suspect certainty indeed for those who saw problems constituted in the overlappings and interstices of multiple worlds. Those princes of problem-solving, mathematicians, know that solving a problem may disclose a world. For those of us who struggled to understand the politics of race and gender, or wondered at the insufficiencies of independence, world-disclosing work on race and sex, colonialism and postcolonialism enabled us if not to solve our problems, at least to know what they are, where they are, and how we might begin to address them.

The refusal of scholars, particularly scholars of postcolonialism, to respect and maintain the boundary between politics and literature provided new directions and new techniques for research on politics.[27] The attention of these workers to work in the humanities enhanced their understanding of structures, strategies, and the mechanics of power. This thesis is principally intended, however, not to chronicle those victories over arbitrary gatekeeping but to open the gates a little wider and to provide guidance to those working in this newly opened terrain.

27. Exemplary works include Benedict Anderson, *Imagined Communities: Reflections on the Origin and Spread of Nationalism* (London: Verso, 1989); Kwame Anthony Appiah, *In My Father's House: Africa in the Philosophy of Culture* (New York: Oxford University Press, 1992); Homi Bhabha, *The Location of Culture* (New York: Routledge, 1994) and *Nation and Narration* (New York: Routledge, 1990); Dipesh Chakrabarty, *Provincializing Europe: Postcolonial Thought and Historical Difference* (Princeton, N.J.: Princeton University Press, 2000); Partha Chatterjee, *The Nation and Its Fragments: Colonial and Postcolonial Histories* (Princeton, N.J.: Princeton University Press, 1993); *Modern Chinese Literary and Cultural Studies in the Age of Theory: Reimagining a Field,* ed. Rey Chow (Durham, N.C.: Duke University Press, 2000); *Selected Subaltern Studies,* ed. Ranajit Guha and Gayatri Chakravorty Spivak (New York: Oxford University Press, 1988); Barbara Harlow, *Resistance Literature* (New York: Methuen, 1987); *Dangerous Liaisons: Gender, Nation, and Postcolonial Perspectives,* ed. Anne McClintock, Aamir Mufti, and Ella Shohat (Minneapolis: University of Minnesota Press, 1997); Uday Mehta, *Liberalism and Empire: A Study in Nineteenth-*Century British Liberal Thought (Chicago: University of Chicago Press, 1999); Timothy Mitchell, *Colonising Egypt* (Cambridge: Cambridge University Press, 1988); Ashis Nandy, *The Intimate Enemy* (Delhi: Oxford University Press); *After Colonialism: Imperial Histories and*

Work in and from literary theory that addresses the status of the author and the license and limits of authority speaks directly to the concerns of social scientists. Authority in politics, as in literature, is more profound, more extensive, more enduring, but also more limited than once was thought. Authority extends as far as the text reaches. This enables the author to transcend spatial and temporal limits. Ibn Taymiyya thus speaks to Sayyid Qutb and continues to have political influence on and through the activities of the political Islamists who rely on his work.[28] The author's power may extend to populations the author never knew or intended to reach. Yet the author does not control the meaning of the text. Nietzsche's contempt for antisemitism reached the eyes but not the minds of his National Socialist readers. The role of the reader has authority.[29] The reader writes the text in reading it: investing it with new referents, uncovering new meanings in it. Some political texts, notably the preamble to the Constitution of the United States, acknowledge this explicitly, making the reader author. Those who read "We the people" are put in the position of authority by that reading. It is they who, within the text, "ordain and establish this Constitution." This recognition has had a profound effect on constitutional scholarship and politics.[30]

Postcolonial Displacements, ed. Gyan Prakash (Princeton, N.J.: Princeton University Press, 1995); Kristin Ross, *Fast Cars, Clean Bodies: Decolonization and the Reordering of French Culture* (Cambridge, Mass.: MIT Press, 1995); Edward Said, *Orientalism* (New York: Pantheon, 1978); Gayatri Chakravorty Spivak, *In Other Worlds: Essays in Cultural Politics* (New York: Routledge, 1998); Gauri Vishwanathan, *Masks of Conquest: Literary Study and British Rule in India* (New York: Columbia University Press, 1989).

28. Ibn Taymiyya was a late thirteenth-/early fourteenth-century Muslim theorist, particularly noted for his justification of war against other Muslims, a justification responsive to the campaigns and conquests of the Mongols. Sayyid Qutb was a twentieth-century Muslim theorist, central to the founding and intellectual development of the Ikhwan al muslimiyya, the Muslim Brothers, a political organization, powerful both in its own right and in its influence on subsequent organizations of political Islamists.

29. Umberto Eco, *The Role of the Reader: Explorations in the Semiotics of Texts* (Bloomington: Indiana University Press, 1984).

30. Robert Cover was among the first to violate the boundary between politics and literature in the study of public law, in *The Public Burning* (New York: Viking, 1977). This boundary violation produced an efflorescence of scholarship

Other texts are, however, not immune to this effect. The reader who interprets the Talmud, hadith, or other legislation assumes a position of authority over those texts and the practices and people they constitute. The ingenious readers who found in the Fourteenth Amendment a variety of rights and powers for developing corporations acquired authority—political and literary—through that enterprise.

This makes the long-hallowed enterprise of seeking "the intention of the author," whether in constitutional interpretation or the history of philosophy, both more difficult and less rewarding than previously thought. This enterprise is more difficult because authority is seen to inhere not only in the first to pen the text but also in others who may have clarified the meaning held within it. It is less rewarding because one is obliged to recognize that the meaning of a particular text is not determined by the one who first penned it. If one can discover, or, more probably, infer, the meaning that the first author intended the text to carry, one is not able then to conclude that this intention governed the unfolding of the text in practice, nor can one argue that this long-expired intent can limit or control the meanings to be found within words that belong to a language (and all the communities that employ that language) rather than to an author.

---

in that field including William F. Harris II, *The Interpretable Constitution,* (Baltimore: Johns Hopkins University Press, 1993); Marianne Constable, *The Law of the Other: The Mixed Jury and Changing Conceptions of Citizenship, Law, and Knowledge* (Chicago: University of Chicago Press, 1994); Owen Fiss, *The Irony of Free Speech* (Cambridge, Mass.: Harvard University Press, 1996); Sanford Levinson, *Constitutional Faith* (Princeton, N.J.: Princeton University Press, 1988); Austin Sarat and Thomas R. Kearns, *Cultural Pluralism, Identity Politics, and the Law* (Ann Arbor: University of Michigan Press, 1999), *History, Memory, and the Law* (Ann Arbor: University of Michigan Press, 1998), and *Law in the Domains of Culture* (Ann Arbor: University of Michigan Press, 1998); *Narrative, Violence, and the Law: The Essays of Robert Cover,* ed. Martha Minow, Michael Ryan, and Austin Sarat (Ann Arbor: University of Michigan Press, 1992). Patricia Williams, *The Alchemy of Race and Rights* (Cambridge, Mass.: Harvard University Press, 1991). This work was, in some cases, notably that of Williams, allied to critical race theory which was itself influenced by the poststructuralism Habermas inveighed against in *The Philosophic Discourse of Modernity.*

10. Culture can be considered as a text.

Cultures, and all people, events, and artifacts within their social worlds, are meaningful: that is, they are full of meaning. One comes to the myriad meanings contained within them as one does in reading a text: by recognizing symbols, locating those symbols in a grammar, and interpreting the resulting texts.[31]

This approach is not without its hazards. Althusser warned against the notion that "one had only to read" the world to understand it.[32] He recognized that construing culture as a text is itself a literary convention with consequences. The world so conceived is always already meaningful, already given to us by God or Hegel. The meaning read in that world may be construed as the work of some author or as a property of the text itself. This attribution of meaning to the world gives it a fictive unity that may not be justified and disguises the authority of the reader of the text and the constitutive power of the interpretive conventions upon which the reader relies. In my view, the warnings Althusser gives authorize the practice. The world we come to, in language, in history, is already full of meaning. The world we must negotiate is linguistic and historical. This is the world we must read.

31. Paul Ricoeur raises the possibility of looking at culture as a system of signs, a network of meaning, a legible text in his essay "The Model of the Text." Ricoeur contends that "the human sciences may be said to be hermeneutical (1) inasmuch as their *object* displays some of the features constitutive of a text as text, and (2) inasmuch as their *methodology* develops the same kind of procedures as those of *Auslegung*, or text interpretation." He delineates a series of features that establish the textual character of the social world, including duration in time, presence, and historicity, and the manner in which meaning is detached from its author and initial location and through this detachment is expanded and deepened. The central contention of this thesis can, however, be distilled in Ricoeur's simple observation that "social reality is fundamentally symbolic." Ricoeur, "The Model of the Text: Meaningful Action Considered as a Text," in *Interpretive Social Science: A Reader,* ed. Paul Rabinow and William Sullivan (Berkeley: University of California Press, 1979), 73–101, 71. Some of those most uneasy with the study of culture may be reassured by Ricoeur's opening statement: "My aim in this paper is to test an hypothesis."

32. Louis Althusser and Etienne Balibar, *Reading Capital,* trans. Ben Brewster (New York: Verso 1997).

The recognition that cultures, or lifeworlds, can be read should not be confused with the idea that each word corresponds to something in the world—or outside it. Quite the contrary. We read the lifeworld, we read our own histories, in our own languages. Wittgenstein cautioned against the view that "proposition, language, thought, world stand in line one behind the other, each equivalent to each." Something is missing there, Wittgenstein argues: "The language game in which they are to be applied is missing."[33] The understanding of culture as a text should not mislead us into the belief that we are placed outside culture, cultures, or language, as readers with mastery over what we read. Language has authority over us. Language constitutes our reading. When we read culture as a text we are engaged in looking at a life, a world, that constitutes those within it, even as we are ourselves constituted by that world (and others). Wittgenstein even provides a particular prayer for this enterprise: "God grant the philosopher insight into what lies in front of everyone's eyes."[34]

If these are the defects of reading culture as a text, they are also its virtues. Reading culture as a text is, in many very ordinary respects, what each of us does every day in order to live in the world.

11. Literary devices have direct counterparts in political strategies.

Compelling illustrations of this thesis can be found quite readily. Metaphor, metonymy, synecdoche, all serve as strategies of authority, in the political as well as the literary sense.

The ubiquity of metaphoric strategies in politics enables them to operate almost unnoticed. Consider how participants in a political discourse confront wars and other conflicts. They warn of "another Vietnam" or the dangers of "appeasement." Palestinians and Contras are compared to "your Founders" or "your Washington

33. Wittgenstein, *Philosophical Investigations*, 96.
34. Wittgenstein, *Culture and Value*, trans. Peter Winch (Chicago: University of Chicago Press, 1984), 63e.

and Jefferson" and their struggles to those of the American Revolution. Earlier wars and conflicts, transformed by discursive practice from conflicts to constellations of symbols and signs, serve as templates for establishing the meaning of emerging struggles whose significance, and moral and emotional valences, have not yet been established. Those urging European and American intervention in the Balkans published photographs and essays likening the Balkan refugees to Jewish refugees of half a century before.

Political figures are likened to established political icons, Arafat becomes Saladin in the struggle over Jerusalem, Nasser and Saddam Hussein become Saladin in confrontations with an invading West. The work of Martin Luther King is legitimated, and its daring and hazards muted, by likening him to Gandhi and Thoreau.

The political effects of metaphor can also be better understood through Roland Barthes's recognition that the sign is not merely a signifier bearing meaning in the signified. Meaning is made through the union of signifier and signified in the sign. Barthes uses the example of roses given as a sign of love, which are neither roses nor passion, but "passionified roses."[35] Love is associated with roses, and roses are associated with love in this practice. Successful metaphoric strategies have reciprocal effects. King is associated with Gandhi, and Gandhi is thereafter associated with King. Where political figures are used as icons of virtue and sources of legitimation, they acquire associations, attachments, and accretions that link them to later figures and events. Their authority extends in time, and in space.

Metonymy may also operate as a political strategy. Many will march under a single banner. A movement—a slogan—will unite diverse pleas, grievances, and demands. These demands may become identified with the experience, actions, agency, or iconic power of a particular class.[36] Marx's account of "merely political" revolutions

35. Barthes, *Mythologies*, 113.
36. Ernesto Laclau writes, "In Italy, during the war of liberation against Nazi occupation, the symbols of Garibaldianism and Mazzinianism functioned as general equivalents . . . as a language which universalized itself by becoming

can also be understood as an instance of (double) metonymy. "For the *revolution of a nation* and the *emancipation of a particular class of civil society to coincide,* for *one* estate to be acknowledged as the state of the whole society, all the defects of society must conversely be concentrated in another class, a particular estate must be looked upon as the *notorious crime* of the whole of society, so that liberation from that sphere appears as general self-liberation."[37] One class comes to stand for all demands, calling up the range of grievances and offenses visited on many.

Political and literary strategies are not readily distinguished, for all are acts of authority. This becomes particularly clear in considering perlocutionary and illocutionary acts, or, as J. L. Austin put it, "how to do things with words."[38] Some words have effects and consequences, and others, more interestingly, do what they say. In these illocutionary acts words are actions, words do. The line between saying and doing, words and actions, vanishes. Wittgenstein put it more abruptly, and more radically: "Words are deeds."[39] The erasure of the (perhaps fictional and misleading) boundary between words and deeds is evident in the Quran, which begins with the command "Recite," and in the Constitution of the United States, where "We the People, of the United States of America . . . do ordain and establish this constitution."

The recognition that political and literary authority are coincident has led a number of theorists, philosophers, and literary and cultural critics to argue for "the violence of the letter."[40] In such ar-

---

the surface of inscription of an increasingly large number of social demands." Ernesto Laclau, in Judith Butler, Ernesto Laclau, Slavoj Zizek, *Contingency, Hegemony, Universality* (London: Verso, 2000), 210, 191, 45.

37. Karl Marx, "Contribution to the Critique of Hegel's Philosophy of Law: Introduction," quoted in Butler et al., *Contingency, Hegemony, Universality,* 45. Italics, Marx.

38. John Austin, *How to Do Things with Words* (Cambridge, Mass.: Harvard University Press, 1962).

39. Wittgenstein, *Culture and Value,* 46e.

40. Jacques Derrida, "The Violence of the Letter," in *Race, Writing and Difference,* ed. Henry Louis Gates (Chicago: University of Chicago Press, 1986).

guments, linguistic acts are read as acts of violence. A declaration of war, a judge's sentence, certain acts of legislation, certain *fatwas,* will be widely and readily acknowledged as illocutionary acts of violence. Other acts, acts of writing and naming that shape identities or foreclose acts and thoughts and forms of life, are seen by a smaller but still significant number as acts of violence, whose power to harm shows the violence at the heart of language.

12. Culture constitutes the body and makes it readable.

This thesis opposes the enduring assumption that bodies are natural, and as natural are outside politics and culture.

Perhaps the best illustration of this comes from Aretha Franklin: "You make me feel like a natural woman." Aretha's praise acknowledges how difficult the achievement of the natural is, how much work goes into it, how dependent it is on conventional categories and the assessment of an other. The woman who says (or sings) "you make me feel like a natural woman" acknowledges that this feeling comes from outside, from another. She is brought, moreover, not to recognize or remember that she is by nature a woman but to feel *as if* femininity were natural to her.[41]

One could also look to the diary of a Indian vicereine who watched naked men bathing and observed that though they were naked, their color made them appear clothed.

One could also look at the work of important painters, photographers, and performance artists whose work recognizes and employs the body as a text. In works by Shirin Neshat, *muhajibat,* or veiled women, are inscribed—on their unveiled faces, their feet, their

41. This reading follows from a conversation about the Aretha Franklin song with Judith Butler and Wendy Brown. See Judith Butler, *Gender Trouble: Feminism and the Subversion of Identity* (New York: Routledge, 1990). Judith Butler's work on gender and sexuality demonstrated that gender was not a natural attribute, but a performance. Butler revealed this by looking at the political as a literary authority. She took a strategy designed to classify and clarify a particular literary form and used it instead to classify and clarify the operation of a particular structural arrangement in politics.

arms. A bare arm emerges from an enveloping *chador,* holding the
hand of a naked child whose body is entirely inscribed. In the film
Irezuma, a woman's body is gradually tattooed in a complex process of inscription uniting sexuality, writing, and violence. Elements
of performance works by Laurie Anderson use light and masks to
inscribe, and in inscribing, gender and race, the performer's body.
Anderson's becomes an Asian body, a male body. Bob Flanagan and
Orlan, among others, have used their bodies as surfaces to be inscribed. Flanagan was a performance artist afflicted with cystic fi-
brosis. The disease imposed suffering on him. In his work, which he
called "supermasochistic," he inflicted suffering on himself.[42] Orlan's most famous series of performances began with the filming of
her own, unpremeditated, surgery. She continued the series with
films of her voluntary cosmetic surgeries. These surgeries altered the
form of her body in order to provide visual commentaries on disparate aesthetic ideals. The last time I checked she had remade herself in the image of figures on Mayan vase paintings.[43] In the work
of these latter artists, transformations of the body alter their character: from passion to action, from external to internal, from imposed to willfully assumed.

13. Gender, race, and sexuality are cultural constructs.

This thesis follows easily from the recognition that culture constitutes
the body and renders it legible. For many scholars, however, the route
of recognition was traveled the other way: recognition of the cultural
construction of race, gender, sex, and sexuality opened the way for
the recognition that the body itself was a cultural construct. Much
of this work was done by scholars of comparative politics. These
scholars were often influenced by anthropology and—still more
often—confronted in the practice of fieldwork with evidence that

42. Flanagan's lifework is documented in the film *Sick: The Life and Death
of Bob Flanagan, Supermasochist* by Kirby Dick.
43. Orlan provides an account of her work, with illustrations, on her Web
site: *www.cicv.fr/creation_artistique/online/orlan/index1.html.*

neither the understanding of racial difference nor racial categories were the same in Brazil, Mexico, and the United States.[44] Outside the Anglo-American academy, both scholars and political actors readily acknowledged W. E. B. Du Bois's famous declaration "the problem of the twentieth century is the problem of the color line."[45] They were conscious as well of the work of Frantz Fanon and C. L. R. James, work that simultaneously foregrounded the problem and interrogated the category of race.[46] Postcolonial scholars explored the construction and performance of racial identities and challenged prevailing conceptions of how one studied and deployed racial categories. They have proposed new temporal and spatial understandings of the world, marking already altered understandings of patterns of cultural community and influence. Within political theory, they revealed the racial politics at work in the nineteenth-century construction of Greece as the natal site of Western political thought.[47]

Within the United States, the work of scholars on race exposed the ambiguities of the concept and its work in the world. Changes in the classification of race over time at one moment cast the Irish as white and at another stigmatized them as simian; such changes also altered the status of Mexicans from white to black and back again. Policy makers puzzled over the categorization of Southern Europeans and Filipinos. Such events revealed the malleability of

44. Michael Hanchard, *Orpheus and Power: The Movimento Negro of Rio de Janeiro and Sao Paolo, Brazil, 1945–1988* (Princeton, N.J.: Princeton University Press, 1994).

45. W. E. B. Du Bois, *Souls of Black Folk* (New York: Modern Library, 1996).

46. Frantz Fanon, *Wretched of the Earth*, trans. Constance Farrington (New York: Grove Press, 1968); *Black Skins, White Masks,* trans. (New York: Grove Press, 1982). C. L. R. James, *Black Jacobins* (New York: Random House, 1989). See also James's essay on cricket and racial politics, *Beyond a Boundary* (New York: Pantheon Books, 1983).

47. Paul Gilroy, *"There Ain't No Black in the Union Jack": The Cultural Politics of Race and Nation* (London: Hutchinson, 1987), *The Black Atlantic: Modernity and Double Consciousness* (Cambridge, Mass.: Harvard University Press, 1993); Michael Hanchard, "Afro-Modernity: Temporality, Politics, and the African Diaspora," *Public Culture* 11, 1 (1999); Martin Bernal, *Black Athena* (New Brunswick, N.J.: Rutgers University Press, 1987).

race in history.[48] The practices of passing (for white) and blackface showed the ambiguity of race in individuals: giving race to the reader as a performance that might be enacted in whole or in part.[49]

Scholars engaged in research abroad and in different social contexts in the United States have also been obliged to be particularly attentive to the cultural construction of sex, gender, and sexuality. The discomfiting recognition that being a man in India, Algeria, or Serbia required a different repertoire of gestures and entailed a different set of privileges and obligations than being a man in the United States might have been less frequently acknowledged in public, but it was difficult to avoid in practice. More recently, scholars in feminist and queer theory have worked to delineate the complex, manifold performances of sex, gender, and sexuality.[50]

48. In addition to Appiah, Gates, Gilroy, Hanchard, Williams, and others already mentioned above, see Cathy Cohen, *The Boundaries of Blackness: AIDS and the Breakdown of Black Politics* (Chicago: University of Chicago Press, 1999); St. Clair Drake, *Black Folk Here and There: An Essay in History and Anthropology* (Los Angeles: Center for Afro-American Studies, University of California, 1990); John Hope Franklin, *The Color Line: Legacy for the Twenty-first Century* (Columbia: University of Missouri Press, 1993); *Drylongso: A Self-Portrait of Black America*, ed. John Langston Gwaltney (New York: New Press, 1993); *Black Looks: Race and Representation* (Boston: South End Press, 1992); Noel Ignatiev, *How the Irish Became White* (New York: Routledge, 1995); Claire Kim, *Bitter Fruit: The Politics of Black-Korean Conflict in New York City* (New Haven: Yale University Press, 2000); *Chicano Politics and Society in the Late Twentieth Century*, ed. David Montejano (Austin: University of Texas Press, 1999); Michael Omi and Howard Winant, *Racial Formation in the United States: From the 1960s to the 1980s* (New York: Routledge & Kegan Paul, 1986); *Black on White: Black Writers on What It Means to Be White*, ed. David Roediger (New York: Schocken Books, 1998); Ramon Saldivar, *Chicano Narrative: The Dialectics of Difference* (Madison: University of Wisconsin Press, 1990); Cornel West, *Race Matters* (New York: Random House, 1994).

49. Michael Rogin, *Blackface, White Noise: Jewish Immigrants in the Hollywood Melting Pot* (Berkeley: University of California Press, 1996); Eric Lott, *Love and Theft: Blackface Minstrelsy and the American Working Class* (New York: Oxford University Press, 1993).

50. Work in feminist theory, women's studies, gender, sexuality, and queer theory has remade intellectual life. This footnote only gestures toward the extent of that literature. *Feminist Genealogies, Colonial Legacies, Democratic Futures*, ed. M. Jacqui Alexander and Chandra Talpade Mohanty (New York: Routledge, 1997); Judith Butler, *Gender Trouble*; Seyla Benhabib, *Situating the Self: Gender, Community, and Postmodernism in Contemporary Ethics* (New York: Routledge, 1992); Cynthia Enloe, *Bananas, Beaches and Bases: Making*

Recognition that race and sex are cultural constructs is not, however, as some still believe, tantamount to dismissing them as epiphenomenal or readily changed. The marks of race and gender can be
considered as texts written on the body, inscribed against the will of
those who bear them. They are difficult to conceal or eradicate, and
erasure only places them *sous rature*.[51] The trace that marks their
nominal eradication preserves them. These signs we bear willingly
or unwillingly may function as stigma, marking their bearers as inferior or dangerous and forcing them to bear costs and burdens not
imposed on others. They may also function as inescapable entitle-
ments, passports to privilege that their bearers cannot set aside or
disavow.[52] Because these marks, these signs, are seen as natural, outside and prior to culture and politics, they are taken as apolitical
and ineradicable. This error comes, in part, from taking the signifier

---

Feminist Sense of International Politics (Berkeley: University of California
Press, 1990); Nancy Fraser, *Unruly Practices: Power, Discourse, and Gender in
Contemporary Social Theory* (Minneapolis: University of Minnesota Press,
1989); Donna Haraway, *Simians, Cyborgs, and Women: The Reinvention of
Nature* (New York: Routledge, 1991); bell hooks, *Talking Back: Thinking Fem-
inist, Thinking Black* (Boston: South End Press, 1989); Luce Irigaray, *This Sex
Which Is Not One*, trans. Catherine Porter with Carolyn Burke (Ithaca: Cornell
University Press, 1985); Denise Riley, *Am I That Name?: Feminism and the Cat-
egory of "Women" in History* (Minneapolis: University of Minnesota Press,
1990); Wendy Brown, *States of Injury: Power and Freedom in Late Modernity*
(Princeton, N.J.: Princeton University Press, 1995); Guy Hocqenghem, *Homo-
sexuality*, trans. Danielle Dangoor (London: Allison and Busby, 1978); Joan
Scott, *Gender and the Politics of History* (New York: Columbia University
Press, 1999); Eve Kosofsky Sedgwick, *Epistemology of the Closet* (Berkeley:
University of California Press, 1990); Gayatri Chakravorty Spivak, *Outside in
the Teaching Machine* (New York: Routledge, 1993); Joan Tronto, *Moral
Boundaries: A Political Argument for an Ethic of Care* (New York: Routledge,
1993); Jeffrey Weeks, *Sex, Politics, and Society: The Regulation of Sexuality
since 1800* (London: Longman, 1989).

51. The concept of *sous rature* is discussed by Jacques Derrida in *Of Grammatology*. That which is placed *sous rature* is like a text that has been crossed
out: the rejected word remains visible underneath at the site of the rejection.

52. See Albert Memmi on "the good colonizer" or "the colonizer who refuses" in *The Colonizer and the Colonized*, trans. Howard Greenfeld (Boston:
Beacon Press, 1991), 19–44.

for the signified, mistaking the physical markers of race and sex for the concepts, costs, and subjectivities they signify.

The burden of bearing a text written on the body has prompted many to see the imposed texts of race and sex as wounds inflicted on the body, as burdens the soul bears, or as chains that bar free movement in the world. They can be. But these are also images in which one sees oneself, standards of performance one aspires to, and identities seized like flags to carry a struggle forward. Racial politics has often carried the banner of race in the vanguard.

14. Commodities serve as semiotic lexicons.

Culture is a network of meaning. Within cultures are other, more specific, networks of meaning. Commodities supply (and engender) needs. They gratify (and engender) desires. Commodities also make silent and persistent communication possible. The semiotic lexicon of dress is perhaps the most ubiquitous. We announce our gender in our dress. We may also announce, sometimes deliberately, sometimes unwillingly and unwittingly, our class, our regional identity, our occupation, our politics, our religion.[53] Even those who profess a profound indifference to dress and ignorance of fashion ("I just dress to be comfortable") can give rapid and sophisticated readings of the clothing of those around them. They can tell which elements are to be taken literally and which are worn ironically. They have learned this capacity for critical reading in practice, for many cultural practices depend on the ability to rapidly and correctly identify the gender, and a contingent array of other attributes, of those one encounters in the world.

People use commodities to read others, and locate themselves, in the social order. The Mercedes and the pickup truck, prints by

---

53. Anne Norton, *Republic of Signs: Liberal Theory and Popular Culture* (Chicago: University of Chicago Press, 1993). See also Arjun Appadurai, *The Social Life of Things: Commodities in Cultural Perspective* (Cambridge: Cambridge University Press, 1986).

Francesco Clemente and Thomas Kinkade, *Pet Sounds, fado,* and the *Goldberg Variations* enable us to orient ourselves in a social field, and they do more. Commodities act as words do: not only as symbols, but as currency. They stand for value, they circulate, and they may be transformed from one form of capital to another. We take the signs of education as currency for education, the signs of social capital secure social standing.[54] Commodities circulate: they are bequeathed to heirs, given to friends, earned, stolen, counterfeited. The subject who serves the right wines or plays the appropriate musical works may buy social—or educational—capital, and the capital thus obtained may be, through a process of exchange, turned to financial advantage.

As currency can be counterfeited, and words can be lies, commodities can also be counterfeit and deceptive.[55] One can (one quite often does) dress to disguise one's class, blurring it in the clothing common to a wide range of classes or assuming articles of clothing that testify to the possession of more financial capital than one may actually have.

In this as in other semiotic lexicons, the signs, like words, can be used in a variety of linguistic strategies. They can be used ironically. One might (Robin Kelley did) read the zoot suit as an ironic commentary on the conventional suit. Signs can make arguments. Gandhi's loincloth and spinning wheel argued for Indian self-rule (in both senses). Signs can quote, they can contain references. Ralph Lauren has referred to the American West and the British Empire, to polo and fox hunting. Alexander McQueen has referred to rap

54. Pierre Bourdieu, *Distinction: A Social Critique of the Judgement of Taste,* trans. Richard Nice, (Cambridge, Mass.: Harvard University Press, 1984). The detail in Bourdieu's analysis demonstrates the precision with which commodities (specific types of music and musical works, furniture, clothing, etc.) enable us to locate subjects in a social field ordered by financial capital, social capital, and educational capital.

55. Jean Baudrillard recognized the role of commodities—particularly dress—in the counterfeiting of social status and explored the political consequences of that strategy. Baudrillard, *Simulations,* trans. Paul Foss, Paul Patton, and Philip Beitchman (New York: Semiotexte, 1983).

and Rastafarianism. Clothing and other commodities can be employed with the same rhetorical strategies that operate in other linguistic venues. Academic recognition came late, but popular practice was already adept at the interpretation of commodities in the discursive practices of everyday life.

15. The natural is a cultural category.

Language (our not-at-all-neutral language) gives nature to us as the counterpart to culture. "I won't play nature to your culture," as a Barbara Kruger composition declares. Language gives nature to us as prior to culture, as that which precedes language.[56] Nature is to be the realm of mere givenness.

Nature is indeed in the realm of mere givenness, but in quite another way. Nature is given to us, in language, in culture, as a category. This category, this condition, this realm, is invested with certain attributes and bound within networks that determine its syntactic limits and link it to other concepts. Perhaps this term and others linked to it—pleasure and pain, needs and rights—enable us to gesture, in language, to what lies beyond it. Perhaps pain and pleasure, needs and rights, are not only presented to us in language but are also only fully present to us there, as linguistic beings. Perhaps we have access to the unmediated given through pain and pleasure. Perhaps pain is finally private. Perhaps pleasure offers the possibility of evading governance and remains an avenue to the immediate and the given, outside regulation. Faith in the accessibility of the given depends on the belief that the sensations of the body are themselves outside culture, outside language. Some regard that claim with suspicion, believing instead that perceptions of pain and pleasure are given to us in language. Others observe that no system is sealed and believe that language, like other systems, must gesture to that which lies outside it.

56. This is an instance of the phenomenon discussed in thesis 90. "Something can come into being as a precondition during or after the emergence of that for which it becomes the precondition."

16. Culture is an observable concept.

This thesis, which I might otherwise have thought too obvious to include, is given in response to "Rule 4.: Maximize concreteness," in *Designing Social Inquiry*. King, Keohane, and Verba place culture among the "abstract, unobserved concepts": "Utility, culture, intentions, motivation, identification, intelligence, or the national interest."[57] In doing so, they run counter not only to generations of work in anthropology, the other social sciences, and much of the humanities but also to Hegel and many who have followed him. In culture, ideas become real in the world. They take on material form and, in doing so, are altered and advanced. Others who might not be conversant with Hegel, or in agreement with his understanding of the relation of the material and the ideal, would nevertheless readily recognize that concepts are observed through and in their material expressions and artifacts. We know concepts from material objects: books and articles. We know concepts as they show themselves in the material world: we see the idea of force in weapons and the bodies of soldiers. We see the state in the documents and institutions of government, in the bodies of those who occupy the physical spaces of governmental offices, and in the practices that governments mandate. Culture is material. Culture is not merely, or even primarily, a set of sentiments, dispositions, or the ideal form of customary practices, a kind of mental template for the world and one's behavior in it. Culture comprises not only precepts but prisons, not only concepts but houses.

King, Keohane, and Verba might reasonably argue that I have mistaken their meaning. By the term *observable* they appear to mean something quite different from the ordinary language meaning of *observation*. They might insist that observation is employed by them as a technical term (what they elsewhere deplore as "jargon") and that observation, in this technical sense, occurs when "we can mea-

57. Gary King, Robert O. Keohane, Sidney Verba, *Designing Social Inquiry: Scientific Inference in Qualitative Research* (Princeton, N.J.: Princeton University Press, 1994), 109–110.

sure the concept independently of the dependent variable we are explaining." Observation in this understanding is a narrow and technical activity, occurring much more rarely than the innocent reader of English might imagine. It is unconnected with sight or any other sense. It is, indeed, a concept whose operation can only be observed indirectly, by means of semiotic indices. Observations are indicated by quantification: only that which has been measured has been observed. This construction casts not only all that cannot be but all that has not been measured into the realm of nonbeing.

The insistence on measurability is allied to the need to maintain the fictive integrity of variables. This can produce fundamental distortions in research design and in the conception of cultural influences. King, Keohane, and Verba furnish a telling illustration in their praise of David Laitin's study of the Yoruba. They quote with approval Laitin's question, "How is one to measure the impact of Islam on a society where nearly everyone is a Muslim?" writing that "Laitin overcomes this problem by turning his research attention to the Yoruba of Nigeria, who are divided into Muslim and Christian."[58] The question is animated by several errant assumptions (apart from the extraordinary hubris of pretending to measure the influence of religion). The research strategy that King, Keohane, and Verba praise assumes that the influence of Islam is confined to Muslims. Yet who could argue that a religion influences only its adherents? Religions in close proximity may influence one another to imitation, differentiation, or a complex series of opposed reactions. Islam will influence (Islam has influenced) institutions and practices shared by Muslims and Christians. The purported elegance of the research design testifies instead to a historical ignorance (of the relations of Muslims and Christians) and a methodological primitivism (concerning the conceptual integrity of variables and the indices of cultural influence) that the lauded author would surely disavow.

58. King et al., *Designing Social Inquiry,* 147. David Laitin, *Hegemony and Culture: Politics and Religious Change Among the Yoruba* (Chicago: University of Chicago Press, 1986).

The narrow construction of "observable" as "measurable" will not succeed in excluding the cultural. A good deal of culture—even the truncated understanding of culture—is measurable in the most literal sense. One can measure tumuli and the length of cell-phone conversations. One can date fossils, paintings, and cultural practices. Measurement of cultural objects and cultural practices is often simpler and more straightforward than the measurement of a "coefficient of disdain" or other methodological arcana.

Ironically, the designation of measurability as the precondition for observation precludes the "maximization of concreteness" at the outset. If we are dependent on measurement, then we are cast from the realm of the concrete and material into the realm of abstraction and semiotics.

Those more familiar with that realm than King, Keohane, and Verba have looked more critically, and with greater rigor, at the enterprise of measurement. The casual identification of measurement with objectivity and scientific neutrality that pervades so much of Anglo-American social science was an early casualty of their studies.

17. Culture is made in practice.

There are many sources for the recognition that culture is made in practice, and many methods and approaches coincide here. One might derive this thesis from Wittgenstein, either directly or from considering the consequences of his views on language. If language is altered in practice, the communal character of language ensures that such practices alter the common.[59] One might also derive it from the empirical work of historians and social scientists who describe alterations in governmental institutions, rituals, methods of punishment, and conceptions of childhood. One could look around. Laws, manners, and fashions change. They change as the people engaged in making, enforcing, violating, and interpreting law; engag-

59. Ludwig Wittgenstein, *Philosophical Investigations,* trans. G. E. M. Anscombe (New York: Macmillan, 1968).

ing with one another; or designing, marketing, or buying clothes conduct these activities. They act within established structures and according to established practices, but they may also (willfully or unconsciously) alter those structures and practices. They repeal laws, they interpret them differently. They choose to *tutoyer* one another, using the informal address as a sign of equality. They blush at bawdy remarks, or they do not. Changes in practice reflect—and effect—changes in principles, values, structures, and conditions. As people change their practices, they change their cultures.

The thesis endorses theories and methods that approach culture as performance. Each culture embraces, in practice, a variety of ways in which social roles can be performed—myriad performances of nationality, gender, class. Each performance differs from the one before. Consider gender. Each performance of the masculine or feminine, of lesbian or gay personae, may alter, slightly or dramatically, not only what it means to be a man or a woman but *how* one is a man or a woman: the repertoire of gestures and inflections that signify feminine or masculine. Each performance may have ironic and unanticipated consequences. Thus Marilyn Monroe alters not only how one may perform the feminine but also how one may perform gay masculinity. Alterations in practice bring change within culture, which leads to the following thesis.

18. Culture, as practice, is continually changing.

The work of practice in changing culture is evident in every aspect of culture. Presidential rhetoric is altered through the practices of presidents as they deliver State of the Union addresses, conduct press conferences, and campaign for reelection.[60] The common law tradition recognizes the effects of practice on rights of way and property rights. Statutory legislation and regulation are altered through their administrative and other practical enactments. These alterations ex-

---

60. Jeffrey K. Tulis, *The Rhetorical Presidency* (Princeton, N.J.: Princeton University Press, 1987).

tend from the material to the ideal. Foucault showed us how the administration, the experience, and finally, the idea of the penitentiary altered in and through the building and administration of penitentiaries.[61] Linguists have shown us how sounds transform over time, and how the spread of reading alters pronunciation. Students of fashion show how practice alters conventions marking gender and class differences. Those who study change in culture have often looked to social history and cultural studies to chart these often inconspicuous but determinative changes.[62]

The recognition that culture is made in practice has important consequences for the study and the strategies of politics. Those without political and economic power can nevertheless find weapons against those who hold dominion over them.[63] They can hide from the tax collector, disguise their holdings, pay the tax in bad currency or rotten grain, steal from their employers and their landlords, walk through or hunt on the lord's fields, or break machines to buy themselves some leisure time. Their small evasions and acts of fraud and sabotage can erode the power of those who oppress them. Illicit appropriations and practices, continued over time, can become tolerated, institutionalized, even acknowledged as rights. These and other instances of resistance through attrition and erosion support Foucault's description of power as diffuse, disseminate, decentralized. They also should provide some consolation to those critics of Foucault who were dismayed at the prospect of power without a central location, and consequently (so they feared) immune from attack. The dissemination of power is attended by the dissemination of resistance. If power is everywhere, so too is resistance. Whatever form power takes, it will be subject to attrition, erosion, and unlooked-for alterations in practice.

61. Michel Foucault, *Discipline and Punish,* trans. Alan Sheridan (New York: Pantheon Books, 1977).

62. Pierre Bourdieu, *The Logic of Practice* (Stanford: Stanford University Press, 1990); Michel de Certeau, *The Practice of Everyday Life,* trans. Steven Rendall (Berkeley: University of California Press, 1984).

63. James Scott, *Weapons of the Weak: Everyday Forms of Peasant Resistance* (New Haven: Yale University Press, 1985). See also Certeau's discussion of *la perruque* in Michel de Certeau, *The Practice of Everyday Life.*

19. The formal is always accompanied by an informal counterpart, the structural by the antistructural and the unstructured.

Recognizing that meaning is created out of difference one knows to look for the opposition, the other. Where there is a center, there is a periphery; where there is a party in power, there is an opposition; where there is power, there is resistance; where there is a government, there are rebels. The recognition and delineation of such binaries is often deprecated, but binarism has a curious tendency to undermine itself. Binaries do not remain stable and limited. They proliferate. The opposite of earth is not only sky but also water, heaven, and space. Man has a binary relation to animal, god, woman, and boy. From these proliferating binaries, one can triangulate particular strategic locations and clarify relations. One can delineate networks of meaning and map particular discursive relations. Work with binaries teaches that no particular binary is exhaustive but that all binaries are productive and dynamic. Within the network of meaning these proliferating binaries compose, certain relations reveal themselves as locally and momentarily inevitable.

Regulations are accompanied by violations and by evasions. The formal economy is accompanied by the informal economy of smuggling, black-marketeering, and barter. Those who study economies should be attentive to these informal and unstructured practices. Those who study law should recognize the importance not only of criminality but also of that which falls outside the law's purview.

The work of symbolic anthropologists like Turner and van Gennep, because it focused on ritual, revealed the dynamic relation between structure, antistructure, and the unstructured. Turner was particularly attentive to the role of the liminal, those who are, in his words, "neither here nor there; they are betwixt and between the positions assigned and arrayed by law, custom, convention, and ceremonial."[64]

Turner understood his work as a counter and corrective to that of Claude Lévi-Strauss. He read Lévi-Strauss as having argued for

64. Turner, *The Ritual Process,* 95.

the primacy of structure, indeed, for structure as all-pervasive. Lévi-Strauss's schema constructed a world of ordered and ordering binaries: up and down, hot and cold, man and woman, and, most famously, the raw and the cooked. Such structures took physical as well as conceptual form, and they exercised a governing power over the formation and the practices of human beings.[65] Turner questioned the stability and universality that Lévi-Strauss ascribed to structure. He recognized that not only do concepts call up their opposites, so too do structures also interpellate antistructures and conceal the presence of the unstructured. These, recognized, could serve as sites where the stability of structure was undermined. Their presence also called into question the structure that Lévi-Strauss had delineated. Each structure might have an other, an alternative, an antistructure, and much might remain outside it.

I came to the recognition of the importance of the unstructured and antistructural through anthropology. There are other ways to this thesis as well. In a later moment, one may be more likely to come to this recognition through literary theory. Derrida takes Lévi-Strauss as his object, brother, and rival in *Of Grammatology*.[66] Derrida, like Turner, questioned the stability and universality of Lévi-Strauss's binaries and recognized that more lay within and outside them. Rousseau was within Lévi-Strauss. In Derrida's reading of Lévi-Strauss's writing lesson among the Nambikwara, colonial structures of authority and deference lay unacknowledged in Lévi-Strauss's education of the natives.

I have cast this thesis, perhaps misleadingly, in relation to structuralism and the responses it evoked from critics within symbolic anthropology and from poststructuralists. The political importance of this thesis becomes clearer if one states it in different terms: structures of power call up structures of opposition and resistance.

65. The importance of linguistic theory to Claude Lévi-Strauss's work is evident throughout. The influence of Ferdinand de Saussure places him in the current that will also carry Derrida. Lévi-Strauss's also bears, in certain of its aspects, a family resemblance to the theories of Noam Chomsky, particularly in its insistence on the neuro-materiality of linguistic structures.
66. Derrida, *Of Grammatology*.

20. Change comes from the liminal.

Not only scholarship, but practical politics, drew attention away from the center to the periphery during the period of anticolonialism and decolonization in Asia and Africa, and in the turmoil of the 1960s in Europe and the Americas. These events made the constitutive role of the periphery visible. Change came to the empire from the colonies, to the metropole from the periphery, to the state from the streets, to old men from adolescents.

This time, these events instructed us to look for change not at the center, but at the periphery. It enabled those who studied politics to recognize the power of liminal, or marginal, groups. These were excluded or, as in the case of the liminal, only partially or ambivalently included in social and political structures and institutions. Nevertheless, they played a significant role in changing structures and institutions. Those who had studied change in ritual began to look for change in politics.[67]

The liminal can become the epicenter of political change. They can work for change themselves. During the Civil Rights movement in the United States, African Americans demanded voting rights, greater inclusion in the institutions of American political and civil society, and a change in the ideas of America and what it meant to be an American. Similar demands from Latinos, Jews, Catholics, women, and gays have altered state, civil, and social structures in the United States. Much earlier, Ibn Khaldun saw this process in arguing that new dynasties emerge from the periphery, where hardship and deprivation hone the talents and cement the solidarity of those at the margins of power. In these processes, those on the boundaries act willfully and on their own behalf.

Liminal groups may also take on central importance as signs rather than agents. Because they stand on the boundaries of identity, they are often central to debates over those boundaries. In antebellum America, as I argued long ago, women, Indians, and African Ameri-

---

67. Victor Turner moved from the study of ritual to the study of politics in *Dramas, Fields, and Metaphors* (Ithaca, N.Y.: Cornell University Press, 1974).

cans marked the boundaries of American identity. Those who argued for extending or contracting those boundaries made diverse use of these liminal groups: identifying themselves with them (as excluded or unjustly subject to another's authority), identifying others with them (as people who ought to be excluded, subjected, or controlled), or using them as signs of American nationality itself. These debates extended from poetry to law, influencing both the legal and informal definitions of American identity. The role of the liminal here was not confined to discourse, for the debates and the operation of this semiotic economy extended into street riots and the Indian and Mormon wars. The primary importance of the liminal was, however, semiotic. They served as signs, even when they acted as agents, and their defining traits were often stripped from them and assumed by others.

21. All cultures are syncretic.

One of the most amusing (and politically forceful) affirmations of this thesis can be found in Daniel Defoe's polemical poem "The True-born Englishman."[68] Defoe, who was responding to critics of William III as a foreign interloper, knew his critics as disingenuous. He argued that the "true-born Englishman" lauded by William's critics was a mongrel, an amalgam of Saxon, Celt, and Norman with a few other things thrown in. Many readily acknowledge the syncretic character of their nations and cultures. Americans mythologize the melting pot. Mexicans name themselves *la raza cosmica,* marking their cultural particularity as an amalgam of Europe, Africa, and the Americas. Germany and Italy remember their modern origins in national alliances of culturally distinct city-states, making Germany and Italy of what once were Saxony and Prussia, Lombardy and Tuscany. Every Algerian wedding and circumcision celebrates a syncretic nationalism, as the bride (or the boy) appears in

---

68. Daniel Defoe, *The True-born Englishman and Other Writing,* ed. P. N. Furback and W. R. Owens (New York: Penguin, 1997).

a series of regional costumes. Every Indian Independence Day is marked by a celebration of constitutive cultural diversity. The Senegalese know the influence of Muslim traders and French colonists, the Peruvians the fusion of Incas and Jesuits. The Japanese recognize the syncretism of the Meiji reforms, and subsequent appropriations of American and European cultural practices and artifacts.

Local cultures know themselves to be syncretic as well. New Yorkers, perhaps the most parochial people on the planet, celebrate New York as the world in small, enfolding waves of immigrants, offering an endless array of once-alien commodities. Small rural towns throughout Southeast Asia fuse Hinduism, Buddhism, and occasionally Islam into distinctive sets of cultural practices.

Initially, it might seem that one could imagine a culture, perhaps a very small one, removed from contact with others, isolated on an island, by mountains or jungle, and consequently "pure." Such imaginings are not uncommon in fiction. They also figure in popular history and anthropology. Hilton's Shangri-La, Montesquieu's Persia, Colin Turnbull's Ik, or Chagnon's Yanomamo present themselves to us as altogether alien. If we must hear of these through a chance traveler or an intrepid anthropologist who has breached the boundary insulating them from the alien, they nevertheless enable us to imagine what they were before the breach, or that another place, as yet unknown to us, might exist.

Such a people, however, would know, more thoroughly and vividly than we, the differences among them. They could not know themselves as a culture. They would know themselves as "the people" or as "people" altogether, the entirety of what it means to be human, or perhaps simply what it means to be. To know themselves as a culture requires knowledge of another, also human and therefore like, but different as well. The very knowledge of that other culture would change their understanding of themselves radically. Once they exhausted the human. Now they were a form of the human. Once they were the people, now they are a people.

A little thought reveals then, that all cultures, even the radically particular and wholly insulated, are syncretic. That which exists as a binding together of people, communities, or other entities, and which exists over time, must be syncretic. Those who are bound together have particular, and varying, understandings of the culture that enfolds them. They understand the culture differently. They perform their identities as cultural subjects differently, for they must relate to a different set of cultural subjects. The culture that exists over time, encompassing generations, contains different people, different minds, different bodies. Much shorter spans of time see the effects of practice in changing culture. Cultures in time are bound to what one might call their own temporal others: to their ancestors, to their posterity, to the culture as it was and will be, in each moment in time.

This is another reason why culture is not a variable. To ascribe autonomy and a hermetic integrity to any culture is to mistake both the particular character of that culture, which derives in part from its relation to others and to its own, and the character of culture as a category of analysis.

22. All cultures are exceptional. No culture is exceptional.

All cultures are exceptional, for each culture is distinctive in certain, continually varying, respects. No culture is exceptional, for all cultures are alike in certain, varying, respects.

This thesis is cast in the form of an abstract assertion. As is often the case with general laws and abstract assertions it has a parochial origin. It is a response to the lingering belief in "American exceptionalism." This faith was a secular expression of the belief that Americans were God's Chosen People, the New Israel. It affirmed that Americans were like no other people, or more specifically that they were manifestly unlike all non-European peoples, and that they were unlike all European peoples in their ability to evade, or inability to establish, the institutions of the social democratic welfare state. Whether American exceptionalism was regarded as a defect or a point of pride, it was understood to constitute a more profound difference than any of those that marked other nations.

This view was unreasonable, but perversely persistent. America was—and is—exceptional, as are all nations and cultures. Assertions of American exceptionalism could not, therefore, be answered with a simple denial. Instead, the critic was obliged to argue that the (often unspecified) exceptionalism that made American exceptionalism more marked than any other lacked that distinction. The isolation of the study of America in the social sciences hid other exceptionalisms from view and prevented their intrusion into debates over American exceptionalism. This exclusion hid, moreover, the intersections, exchanges, and circulation that linked American cultures to others.

The second part of this thesis, the contention that no culture is exceptional, is a bit of a risk, and a bit of a cheat, but useful nevertheless. The contention is risky because the abstract universality of the claim makes it finally defensible only in those sophistical terms that are a bit of a cheat: no culture is wholly exceptional because our capacity to recognize it as a culture is dependent upon the recognition of likenesses between it and other, already recognized cultures. The thesis is useful nevertheless because it spurs one to look not only for the differences between cultures but also for the sites of likeness and the instances of borrowing, circulation, and exchange that may exist between them.

23. Culture is wild and various.

No culture can be monolithic, because all cultures are syncretic. No culture can be monolithic, because structures entail the antistructural and the unstructured. Cultures instead are wild and various: producing the hybrid and alien, cultivating variations as they grow, change, and remain the same.

Syncretism links cultures to one another, rendering their boundaries porous and uncertain. A figure like Menachem Begin or Levi Eshkol becomes a gate from the Mediterranean to Europe. The Palestinians who say "the cousins are coming for a visit" to warn of an impending Israeli military incursion stand at another gate. Islam is of Arabia, Africa, Indonesia, Europe, and the Americas. Egypt is of Africa and the Orient, of the Pharaohs and Islam. Even those things understood as most one's own may undermine rather than reinforce the particularities of cultural identity. Roland Barthes's iconic French meal, *steak et frites*, is as American as apple pie.[69] One might picture a culture as a Web page, containing a set of links, each opening a gate to that which is at once one's own and a link to others. In culture, as in language, meaning is made out of difference.

The constitutive differences of identity, bound in a syncretic unity, nevertheless ensure that there will be differences within a culture. Those who see Egypt as Pharaonic oppose themselves to those who see it as Muslim. Those who see America as the City on the Hill oppose themselves to those who see it as the New Rome. These opponents will be bound together by a common land, coincident or contending histories, and, most firmly, by their opposition.

The opposition of contending elements in a cultural constellation need not fragment or fracture a culture. They may bind the contending parties more closely to one another. They ensure, however, that no culture is monolithic. A similar insurance is furnished by the operation of structure. Structures interpellate antistructures. Governments evoke opposition. Norms of behavior call forth the aberrant, the inverted, the perverse.[70] The resistance that is entailed in structure and dominion ensures that cultures always contain within themselves critical points of vantage. The claim, still curiously current among Anglo-Americans and Europeans, that critique is peculiar to the West is thus the most errant nonsense. In the absence of investigation of the disparaged culture, a little consideration of the workings of structure or the character of collective identity would dispel this.

Cultures are, moreover, present in the people that comprise them. They are performed. These people, differently constituted and dif-

69. Barthes, *Mythologies*, 62–64.
70. The locus classicus for this observation is Michel Foucault, *History of Sexuality*, vol. 1. It is a recurrent theme in Foucault's work, and it has influenced a wide array of critical work on the normal, the aberrant, and the perverse.

ferently placed, conceive and perform their cultures differently. They
too ensure, in and through their practice, that no culture is monolithic.

24. Subjects have multiple identities.

The concept of the individual, like the word itself, argues for a notion of the subject as indivisible, a single being. This thesis opposes
that conception. Subjects are manifold, containing constellations of
identities. Each of us has avatars.

One can come to this understanding through several different critiques of the idea of the individual. One reading of the thesis would
simply urge recognition that a given subject may have markedly different identities in different contexts. Thus a woman might be identified, by herself and others, as a mother at home, and as a lawyer
in the office. She might even be called by her husband's name when
acting in the domestic sphere, while assuming a different name in
the course of her professional work. Another subject might act with
the loyalties, and according to the preferences and norms of his
identity as a Jew in one instance, while being moved by a different
set of norms, preferences, and loyalties when acting as a Democrat.
The combination of desires, imperatives, and constraints that accompany each identity may be in accord or in conflict. If they conflict in principle, they may or may not have occasion to conflict in
practice. The strategic interaction of identities in an individual is,
however, important political terrain. It is necessary to remember that
individuals figure in politics not simply as pieces on a board or as
those moving the pieces but also as the elements of the board.

The critique of the individual fielded in this thesis can take on a
more radical form. In this reading, which I endorse, the recognition
of multiple identities in a nominal individual undermines prevailing
constructions of individuality, including some of the most commonplace and powerful. Many understandings of the individual, for example, mark bodily integrity as not only the sign but the substance

of the individual. For Wittgenstein, the sensations of the body and the particularities of thought and appetite were ultimately private and incommunicable. If one was not closed within one's body, there were nevertheless reaches of that space and the understanding it enclosed that remained wholly private. Innumerable conventions encourage the belief that one is one's body, or in a more spiritual variant, in one's body. We are, as Lacan recognized, called to occupy our bodies, an occupation we experience as a triumph of the will and meet with *jouissance*.[71]

Derek Parfit and Thomas Schelling are among those critical of the assumption that the body gives one singularity.[72] Both have observed the tendency of sensation to undermine the nominal integrity of the embodied self. The appetites and sensations of the body vary radically over time, undermining the capacity of the embodied individual to maintain a willful or conceptual unity over time. Parfit also observes that the body has multiple forms in youth and age, sickness and health. The cells that make up the body—that is, the body's material substance—may change completely over the course of an ordinary life span, so that the aged individual has neither the form nor the substance that belonged to that individual (if it was that individual) in youth.

The conception of subjects as internally divided has a longer, and quite canonical, history. Plato fielded several myths of the self divided. In the *Symposium*, he has Aristophanes argue that "each of us bears like a flatfish, the traces of having been cut in two." Aristophanes' myth ascribes human sexuality to an earlier division, which has left each searching for that which would restore a lost whole-

---

71. Jacques Lacan, "The Mirror Stage," in *Ecrits*, trans. Alan Sheridan (New York: W. W. Norton, 1977). Anne Norton, *Reflections on Political Identity* (Baltimore: Johns Hopkins University Press, 1988), 13–14.

72. Derek Parfit, *Reasons and Persons* (Oxford: Oxford University Press, 1984); Thomas Schelling, "Ethics, law and the exercise of self-command," in *The Tanner Lectures on Human Values IV*, ed. S. McMurrin (Salt Lake City: University of Utah Press, 1983), 43–79; and Thomas Schelling, *Choice and Consequence* (Cambridge, Mass.: Harvard University Press, 1984); *The Multiple Self*, ed. John Elster (Cambridge: Cambridge University Press, 1986).

ness.[73] Freud too saw the individual as fundamentally divided. The Freudian divisions of ego, id, and superego have become commonplace. Freud's account doubly undermines the integrity of the individual: by postulating a divided self and by providing an account of the presence of the other (convention, civilization, and the father consumed) within it.[74]

25. Identities are performed.

This thesis refers to both collective and individual identity. In each case, the recognition of identities as performed enables—or obliges—one to recognize them as made from, and containing, difference, as multiple and manifold in their singularity.

Consider collective identities. There are many ways to be American, or Mexican, or Japanese. The historical models for American identity furnished by Abraham Lincoln, Malek al Shabazz, J. P. Morgan, Mother Jones, Billy Graham, Marilyn Monroe, and Allen Ginsberg differ radically, yet all are not only recognizably, but also vividly, American. Being Mexican can refer to the Spanish or the Aztecs, Emilio Zapata or la Guadalupe. The performances of national identities like these are often inflected by race, region, religion, or class, and they are nearly always gendered. Within a given historical moment Egyptian is performed differently by Gamal Abd al' Nasser and Zeinab al Ghazali, Sayyid Qutb and Umm Khalthoum.

---

73. Plato, *Lysis, Symposium, Gorgias,* trans. W. R. M. Lamb (Cambridge, Mass.: Harvard University Press, 1975), 141. For commentaries on this and additional arguments on the splitting of the once-individual, see Jacques Lacan, *Four Fundamental Concepts of Psychoanalysis,* trans. Alan Sheridan (New York: W. W. Norton, 1978), 197; Anne Norton, *Reflections on Political Identity,* 11–49.

74. Sigmund Freud, *Totem and Taboo,* trans. James Strachey (New York: W. W. Norton, 1950), *Group Psychology and the Analysis of the Ego,* trans. James Strachey (New York: W. W. Norton, 1959). Freud's account of the self as fundamentally divided becomes central to psychoanalysis and psychoanalytic theory and consequently appears, in altered forms, in the work of Melanie Klein, Carl Jung, Karen Horney, and other seminal figures.

The performance of nationality, as this list indicates, will often (if not always) entail political positions and have political consequences. Deliberate, willful performances of collective identity incorporate historical references, make arguments, and provide commentaries on the character and direction of the whole. No single performance exhausts the repertoire of what it means to be American, Israeli, Australian, or Japanese.

Gender is itself a performance.[75] Maria Callas, Flo Jo, Eleanor Roosevelt, Marilyn Monroe, Margaret Thatcher, Divine, RuPaul, and Cruella De Vil all performed the feminine. One can perform the feminine as babe, belle, butch dyke, bitch, or bluestocking, and there is always room for improvisation. Perhaps more importantly, no performance is necessarily determinative, though convention may oblige subjects to act as if it were so.

The performative character of individual identity gives a new and revelatory resonance to the term "rational actor." For those mindful of the performative, the emphasis falls not on "rational" but on "actor" and reminds us that even the most interested and intended action entails other forms of acting. *Acting for* a particular object involves *acting for* a particular audience. In *acting as* a rational subject, one is *acting* a particular social role. Here, as in other instances of simulation, the map precedes the territory, the role calls forth the performance.[76]

The discourse of variables and the habits of thought that go with it rely upon stable units and categories. Liberal theory and liberal practice interpellate individuals whose individualities are equivalent, if not identical. Popular culture instructs one to "be yourself" and rewards certain choices of costume with the praise "it's you!" High culture preaches "to thine own self be true." Popular culture, high culture, the political institutions of liberalism, and the requirements of methods employing the discourse of variables all tend to support the idea of identity as an internal homunculus whose will,

75. Butler, *Gender Trouble.*
76. Baudrillard, *Simulations.*

judgments, and appetites are prior to politics. Yet these cultural sources also supply critiques of the idea of an internal, singular, and entirely autonomous self. Perhaps most importantly, the ordinary practices of daily life school us to recognize the changes of costume that go with changes of role and to recognize ourselves as engaged in performances in expressing the most constitutive components of individual identity.

26. Identities have multiple expressions.

No performance is quite like any other.[77] Each performance of a role, or an identity, alters it, for repetition always alters the repeated. Writing one's fifth book or jumping one's thousandth fence is not the same as the first. A repeated gesture or a repeated donation can evolve from impulse to habit. This thesis can also follow from the recognition that subjects have multiple identities. Ruhollah Khomeini was an *alim*, a poet and a revolutionary, father, husband, and exile. He expressed these identities by writing philosophy, poetry, and polemics, by inciting insurrection, and by other private and public actions in Iran and abroad. An array of practices follows from each fragment of the bundled identities that settle under the rubric of a name.

Work on identity once took each identity as a unit. One asked how personal identity was formed, or how one national identity differed from another. Through these endeavors, one learned to ask how each national identity differed not only from others but within, and from, itself. One learned to think of the formation of personal identity in reverse: "how one becomes what one is" and "not to discover who we are but to refuse who we are."[78] These questions, now

77. The film *Diva*, by Jean-Jacques Beineix (1982), based on the book *Diva* by Delacorta (New York: Ballantine, 1983) is predicated on the unique character of performance.

78. Nietzsche, *Ecce Homo, Foucault Live*, trans. John Johnston, ed. Sylvere Lotringer (New York: Semiotexte, 1989).

being asked by those who work on identity, must be asked throughout the discipline.

In the meantime, this thesis and those that preceded it suggest some techniques for work on and among identities. Each subject has several identities. Each identity is partial and manifold. Each identity is performed. Subjects can not only be seen but also can be precisely (if contingently) delineated, as changing constellations of identity. One can ask which identities are operative in which contexts, at which places, at which times, for which audiences, for which ends. One can ask how a particular identity is expressed: with what gestures, through which media. One can ask how the performance of a given identity creates it and changes it in time and space. These are all researches that map subjects in time and space, and in relation to others. These maps indicate complex relations within and between identities. As these are mapped, one can begin to investigate how this complex terrain is negotiated and to explore the strategic possibilities that particular configurations of identity open and preclude.

27. Every identity is in reference to a collective.

This thesis is most readily accepted with regard to collective identities. Most ordinary statements of identity, from "I am an American" to "I am a vegan," make reference to a broader community. In taking the name, claiming the identity, the speaker refers to a collective, most commonly an encompassing community. Identities constructed in negation have the same effect. Those who asserted "I am not and have never been . . ." constructed themselves as outside, apart from, and against the Communist Party of the United States.

The collective character of identity is also true, however, for more particular and seemingly private identities. Not only party memberships and professional and occupational identities but religion, race, marriage, and sexuality are constructed in relation to collectives. This construction is, as the examples suggest, formal and institutional, informal and customary, on paper and in practice, as well as conceptual. The most particular identities, those that individual subjects craft for themselves, the internal visions they have of themselves, the performances they give of their identities as they conceive them, are also in relation to collective identities. The man who sees himself as a cowboy, a rebel, a descendant of Scotch-Irish immigrants links himself to elements of American, Scottish, and Irish national imaginaries. The most intimate identities appeal to histories, myths, and literatures belonging to nations and other collectives.

Individual identity is constructed in and through institutions and markets as well as history and myth. For Althusser one comes to certain identities, or if you prefer, social roles, through a process called interpellation.[79] (I prefer Althusser's alternate expression "hailing," but "interpellation" seems to have caught on.) Althusser presents us with a fable of the quotidian: the policeman calls out "Hey you!" and you turn around. This episode from the everyday captures one of the ways in which identity is most commonly formed. You are called by a name, and you answer to it. One is hailed as a man or woman, black or white. Catalogs interpellate gardeners, hunters, athletes. Journalists interpellate Yuppies and New Democrats. The state interpellates criminals, citizens, taxpayers, voters, welfare recipients. Recognition of this phenomenon has facilitated work on the role of institutions in the creation, continuance, and amendment of identity.

The construction of identity in and through community has readily recognized dimensions in time and space. It is on this collective dimension of identity that one most easily sees the link between identity and historicity. Belonging to a community links one to the dead and the unborn. One has a past, as an American, as a German,

---

79. Louis Althusser, "Ideology and the Ideological State Apparatus," in *Lenin and Philosophy and Other Essays* (New York: Monthly Review Press, 1971), 127–68. See also Judith Butler's essay on Althusser in *The Psychic Life of Power* (Stanford, Calif.: Stanford University Press, 1997).

as a Latino, as a Jew. One is bound in and to histories held in common. One has an inheritance of practices and rituals. One has ancestors. One also has posterity. Collective identity extends one's being into the future as well as the past. These collective identities are commonly given place in a land or region. They are linked to a particular site or space, and presence within that space puts one in the presence of that identity as it extends over time.

28. Identity and community are coeval.

Individual and collective are related, in Aristotle's phrase, "as concave is to convex." Here it is the dimension of time that is at issue.

For a given individual, mindful of the process of interpellation, conscious of identity as something given by experience and imagination from, and within, communities, identity follows community in time. For most people, most of the time, identity is thought to be an inheritance. One belongs to a community much older than oneself. Belonging to that community gives one ties to that past, an inheritance from it, obligations to it.

We might learn to question this understanding. The past is not past, but in the present. There may be many pasts in a single moment of historical presence. Disraeli's past as an Englishman was not Gladstone's. Perhaps we can learn to locate those pasts in the time of their conception, and in the times in which they conceived their subjects. Perhaps we will learn how to better understand, or more clearly express, the presence of the past in time. There is also the question of conception. Those who believe themselves to be formed in the past look for that past within themselves. Are their pasts then coeval with them? Are they self-generating?

Whatever the experience of particular individuals, the idea of individuality, the category of the individual, and individuals conscious of themselves as such are born at the same moment as collective identities. Collective identities entail the concept and the practice of individuality. The idea of America, and the Americans that it comprises, are born of the same conception. The concept of the community makes membership in it possible. The individuals who belong to it give the community presence in the world. Whether or not there are particular individuals to incarnate the idea of community, the idea of the individuals whom the community will comprehend appears at the same moment, and in the same conception, as the community.[80]

29. Identity and alienation are coeval.

The individual is simultaneously a part of and apart from the community. One is, as an individual, a member of one or more communities. One is a part of each of those communities. One is also, as an individual, apart from the community. The community acknowledges, indeed, constitutes, the distinctions that separate individuals from one another, and from the whole. As the ideas of individuality and community are entailed in one another and necessarily come into being simultaneously, so too do belonging and alienation. As one knows oneself to belong to a community, one also knows oneself to be distinct from it, partial: apart from it exactly because one is only a part of it. The individual is not adequate to the community. The community is not adequate to the individual. Each person exceeds the community, having traits, doing work, willing, acting, thinking, in ways that go beyond the bounds of the community.

30. Every political institution calls for identities.

Politics is a vocation in the fullest sense. Political institutions convoke, provoke, and evoke collective and individual identities. They have officers and staff, people who understand themselves, and are understood by others, to act as or on behalf of the institution. The police department makes police officers, the armed forces make sol-

80. Norton, *Reflections on Political Identity*, 11–14.

diers and sailors. The Constitution creates senators and representatives, Congress constitutes congressional staffers. Less formally, but no less effectively, the Republican Party makes Republicans, the Democratic Party, Democrats. Other identities are also called into being by political institutions.

Institutions call up and constitute not only the identities of those who act in and as the institution but also of those the institution acts upon. This is done, in the first instance, through the effects of categorization. Thus the Bureau of Indian Affairs made "Indians" of a group of disparate and warring tribes. Taxation creates not only tax farmers and tax collectors, but taxpayers. The effects of these structures of governance on identity are often profound. They can be found even where a political institution understands itself as governing—or even simply recognizing—extant identities. One much studied set of examples concerns the effects of the government of India on caste, linguistic, and religious identities.[81] The institutions of colonial governance had important effects on these identities even where they deliberately sought to avoid intervention. British colonial policy generally deprecated assimilation, preferring a policy of recognizing (and governing) existing communities. This policy required political institutions charged with identifying those communities and codifying their beliefs and practices. The categories employed for this purpose—religion, for example—were derived from previous British experiences and understandings. Applying these categories led to misunderstandings and misrepresentations of those categorized. More importantly, as governance was carried out through these categories, subjects found themselves obliged to accord to them in a variety of official and informal discourses. The National Archives of India and the India Office Library in Britain are full of documents in which the British argue to an unpersuaded Hindu, that Hindu practice requires (or forbids) a particular prac-

81. For the influence of British policy on caste, see Lloyd and Susanne Rudolph, *The Modernity of Tradition* (Chicago: University of Chicago Press, 1967). The effects of British colonial policy on religious identity are frequently remarked, particularly with regard to the partition of India and Pakistan, and may be found in most general histories of the subject.

tice or form of dress. My personal favorites are contained in a memorandum entitled "The Much-Vexed Shoe Question." Similar instances are known to every student of colonial policy.

The constitutive effects of institutions go beyond their agents and subjects to the creation of other occupations and identities. Taxation creates not only tax collectors, tax assessors, and taxpayers but also lawyers specializing in taxation. The identification of a particular category of people, identity, or dimension of identity calls forth not only those who will govern, but also those who will study. Political institutions interpellate scholars and scholarship, those whom they govern, and those who resist governance.

31. Identities make interests. Interests make identities.

The first element of this thesis, that interests follow identities, emerged as an important caveat to those social scientific methods, like rational choice, that delineated particular strategic situations consequent on the pursuit of interest. Scholars realized that a rational choice might differ according to the subject's ends and social constraints. They might also have realized, though for the most part they did not, that rationality is also entailed in identity, and that culture determines the calculus by which a subject determines interest. The choice and the rationality in rational choice were artifacts of particular systems and structures. A given rational actor would choose within those structures, using the reasons and the reasoning they made available. This does not, however, produce a single set of limits for each actor or each choice.

A given subject may have access to more than one cultural system: more than one system of rationality, more than one set of interests. Consider a choice concerning medical treatment. The subject may reason as a Catholic, as a mother, as a scientist. These identities, comprised in a single person, entail different ends, different licenses and constraints, different imperatives, and often different rationalities and different interests.

The second element of the thesis, that interests interpellate identities, derives from the thesis just discussed. One of the ways in which political institutions interpellate identities is through the creation of interests. As agencies create benefits, they also create an interest in obtaining those benefits. Those with an interest in obtaining the benefits must cast themselves as the recipients envisioned by the agency's mission, agenda, and regulations. These interests and the identities that respond to them can be created by judicial bodies as well as through legislation and regulation. In the United States, decisions on compensation and the return of lands have created local interests in tribal identities. As this has happened, some tribes have altered and regularized the determination of tribal identity to facilitate recognition or to limit the numbers of the tribe. Decisions on equal protection and Title 9 have encouraged, and in some cases created, populations of female athletes and have given more salience to that identity.

32. There are no "interests." There are "interests of" and "interests as."

There are still a few literatures where people write casually of "interests." This lack of qualifications is a sign of the firm conviction that the interests in question are already known, and can be of only one kind. This use of the term *interests* is symptomatic of views holding that all features of identity but one—commonly, material interest—are epiphenomenal.

The recognition, across the otherwise hostile terrain of contending methods, that interests follow identities carried with it the recognition that there were not interests in the abstract, but the particular interests of particular people.

The recognition that identities were, in practice, contingent, partial, multiple, and multifaceted prompts the second qualification. A single subject may have interests as a citizen, a father, a taxpayer, a farmer. These interests may coincide, or they may not. They will, in either case, constitute a strategic field in which the subject negotiates the demands of a complex identity.

These recognitions have led to the asking of two sets of questions. Claims regarding interests prompt questions about those interests. Whose interests are they? From what do they derive? This set of questions drives critiques, making underlying assumptions visible and subjecting them to critical examination. The second set of questions drives research. They have led scholars to look for contending interests in a single subject, to map hierarchies of interest and preferences, to ask what makes a subject's interest as, for example, a farmer rather than a taxpayer triumph in a particular situation.

Interests are derivative of identities, but not invariably so. In some cases, as the previous thesis argued, interests create identities. Often both phenomena will be at work simultaneously. It is not an object but an error to look for a single direction of causation in the relation of identity and interest. What is important is to insist that those who refer to "interests" qualify that term, for that added precision is required for rigor in research and identifies new questions and new fields for investigation.

33. Every identity is partial.

This thesis is deliberately ambivalent, for identities are partial in both senses of the word. Each identity is incomplete, for it depends upon a relation to a collective of which it is a part, and from which it stands apart. Each identity entails preferences, prejudices, biases, inclinations.

"Civil man," Rousseau wrote, "is only a fractional unity, dependent on his denominator; his value is determined by his relation to the whole, which is the social body."[82] Whether that whole is a polity or the entirety of humanity (what Marx termed "species being"), involvement in it is an acknowledgment of individual incompleteness. Lacan, like Plato, saw human incompletion as entailed in sexuality.

---

82. Jean-Jacques Rousseau, *Emile, or On Education,* trans. Allan Bloom (New York: Basic Books, 1979), 40.

The individual is rendered incomplete by having lost "what the sexed being loses in sexuality."[83] Desire for the sexual other, or knowledge of the conventional division of one's kind into two sexes, apprises the individual that incompleteness belongs to individual identity.

Many other accounts delineate the incompleteness entailed in identity. Hegel's account of the dependence of the identity of the master on the servant draws attention to another sense in which each identity is partial. Each identity is dependent on those others against which it defines itself. Each of these recognitions of the incompletion that identity entails has political implications.

Identities also entail partialities. One is not only a part of one's kind, one is also partial to it. Identities entail prejudices and inclinations. These are often manifest in what one takes for granted, and what one cannot not want.

Plato and Freud both give accounts of individual identity as fundamentally divided. Plato's version of this thesis runs, "Each of us bears like a flatfish the traces of having been cut in two." Rousseau observed that the citizen was at once sovereign and subject. He also argued that in belonging to a community, the individuals who constitute it divide themselves. They belong to the community, and they are, as individuals, distinct from it. Their entry into a larger, more comprehensive form of being divides each of them.

34. Community entails alienation.

Community, therefore, entails alienation. The individuals who join the community are made at once more general and more specific. Each is a part of the community and apart from it. Each experiences a more comprehensive form of belonging, and in the very recognition of the terms of that belonging, each experiences the recognition

---

83. Jacques Lacan, *Four Fundamental Concepts of Psycho-Analysis,* trans. Alan Sheridan, ed. Jacques-Alain Miller (New York: W. W. Norton, 1978), 197. I discuss this more extensively in *Reflections on Political Identity,* chapter 1.

of those features that make the individual distinct from the community. The recognition of those distinctive traits that individuality comprises alienates the individual. The very process that enhances identification with the community enhances alienation as well. As the individual becomes conscious of likeness to the community, the individual also becomes conscious of those traits that preserve individuality.

35. Belonging may be expressed as affirmation or rebellion.

The American who pierces her tongue, travels to Cuba, and refuses to vote is as American as the corporate mogul who raises funds for the Republican Party when he's not playing golf at the club. Each will be claimed by some, disavowed by others, and recognized by all within the cultural system. The Japanese *bosozoku* of the 1980s belonged to Japan as thoroughly as the salaryman. Dick Hebdige's study of subcultures understands them as both British and rebellious, with the particular styles of these rebellions becoming practices in a distinctively (and self-consciously) British repertoire.[84]

Political rebellion, even when it takes the form of secession or armed resistance to the state, may understand itself as adherence to a cultural identity. The rebellious states of the Confederacy retained the name "American" and most of the text of the Constitution, insisting that their rebellion expressed allegiance to national principles. Members of militia movements seeking to overthrow the present regime, and, in some cases, engaged in armed resistance to the government, have frequently insisted that they are the true Americans, and that their rebellion is an expression of allegiance.

All cultures contain many roles. Some of those may be marked simultaneously as rebellious and as fully expressive of cultural (or even national) identity. This is, in part, the work of history. Some figures regarded at one time as outside the culture may be brought

84. Dick Hebdige, *Subcultures: the Meaning of Style* (London: Methuen, 1979), *Hiding in the Light* (London: Routledge, 1988).

within it—even to sites of cultural centrality. More often, figures will be cast even in their own time as rebellious but nevertheless as belonging to the community. Time and changing circumstances may mute the threat they once posed, and as the danger declines, the figure's cultural identity becomes less ambiguous and more readily and broadly accepted.

Cultures contain many recognitions of the rebel as belonging. Western outlaws and Chicago gangsters are icons of American identity. Australians claim Ned Kelly, the English claim Robin Hood.[85] Jack Kerouac and the rebels of the Beat Generation have become American icons. Films have followed the older traditions of stories and ballads in claiming as their own rebels, loners, and the alienated. Those on the boundaries exist in a zone of ambiguity, calling up not only what it is to be American or Australian or Japanese but also what an American or Australian or Japanese might desire, long for, love, pursue, or one day dare to be.

36. Each institution calls for its own resistance.

Taxation interpellates not only tax collectors and taxpayers but also tax exiles and tax resisters. As an institution operates in the world, providing goods, regulating practices, enforcing, incarcerating, curing, teaching, it makes the ideas and the powers that animate it visible. As these become visible, they become objects of either affirmation or rejection. As institutions make authority active, they also make it accessible. The government that touches you can be touched by you. Soldiers sent to a neighborhood make an occupation visible and immediate, but they also provide an incarnation of the occupying power, a target for those who set themselves against the occupation.

Rebels are instructed in resistance by those who rule and exploit them. Each practice of exploitation marks a site of resistance and often suggests the manner in which the powerful are to be resisted.

85. Eric Hobsbawm treated Robin Hood and explored the political significance of rebellions of this kind in *Primitive Rebels* (New York: Praeger, 1963).

If there is a tax on tea, the tea can be thrown into the harbor. If there is a tax on salt, salt can be made from the sea. If machines take labor from workers or diminish their wages, machines can be sabotaged or their breakdowns celebrated. If workers are held to a schedule or punch a time clock, the time clock can be attacked. If the West—or the government—deprecates the *hijab*, the *hijab* can be worn against the government, or against the West. Subaltern groups of many kinds have followed similar strategies in letting institutions guide the forms of their resistance.

Institutions are multidimensional. Governmental institutions manifest the power of the state as well as particular objects of government and particular means toward those objects. They may therefore interpellate resistance on any or all of these dimensions. This makes it necessary for researchers to look carefully at resistance and attempt to articulate the particular aspect of the institution that is the object of resistance. As this suggests, resistance movements, or even particular local acts of resistance, may comprise disparate, even opposed, practices, forms, and objects. Draft resistance, for example, may unite pacifists with those opposed to conscription, and with those opposed to neither conscription nor war in general but to the particular war being conducted or the state conducting it. Studying the diverse resistances interpellated—and joined together—by a given institution thus provides an avenue for research into the operation of coalition politics.

Theorists may recognize this thesis as a consequence of the creation of meaning through difference, articulated on the plane of institutional politics.

37. There is no culture without resistance.

Cultures call forth resistance both internally and externally. The economy of allegiance and resistance maintains the external boundaries of a given culture and gives it its internal articulation.

Allegiance to a common identity entails separation from all others, rejection of some, enmity to others. Being French, for example, precludes being English or Thai and may involve, at certain moments and in certain contexts, enmity to the German or the American. Cultural identity is established (though not solely) through negation. In being French, one is not American, not Thai. Much useful work has been done on the role of the other. Others, however, take more forms and enable more relations than those of rejection and enmity. The other may be the enemy, the other may be an object of contempt or loathing. A good deal of valuable scholarship has detailed the many and subtle ways in which the other is constructed to serve the self. Demonizations of the other are particularly common in wartime, or where they mirror divisive differences within the culture.[86] The other may also be an object of desire, marking a lack or inadequacy in the culture one acknowledges as one's own. The young Americans who traveled to India in the 1960s came as pilgrims, persuaded that India held spiritual powers and practices alien to the West. For these people, the other was an object of desire, emulation, and aspiration.

Living within a culture entails a complex of relations to its practices and institutions. A subject will admire some iconic cultural figures and despise others, adopt some practices, reject others, affirm some institutions, oppose others. The cultural identity of each individual is fashioned through these negotiations of networks of meaning and materiality. These negotiations fashion individual identities from and within an economy of acceptance and rejection, accordance and resistance.

These two dimensions can also be negotiated in relation to each other. Those who stand as others to one's culture provide to the resistant within it possible sites of alternative identification or places of evocative exile. Gertrude Stein takes up the life of an American in Paris, W. E. B. Du Bois ends his life in Ghana. Contending parties within a culture may identify their adversaries with the enemy and the alien, arguing against their inclusion. Those contending for a more expansive polity or culture may claim members of other cultures as their kin, actually or metaphorically.

86. Michael Rogin provides a useful account of the mechanism of demonization in *Ronald Reagan: The Movie and Other Episodes in Political Demonology* (Berkeley: University of California Press, 1987). Freud's writings on paranoia are also useful in this regard.

38. There is no culture without internal critique.

Resistance, as we saw in the previous thesis, maintains the external boundaries and internal structure of cultures. In light of this, it might seem unnecessary to include this thesis. I do include it in response to a curiously persistent insistence by some European scholars that the capacity for self-critique has developed only in the West.

Cultures provide internal critiques in and through the forms of resistance they interpellate. These resistant identities and actions offer practical critiques of that which they oppose. Internal critiques are not, however, confined to the practical outside the West. Cultures are conceived, articulated, given literary expression, described, and lauded by their own. These, like other cultural practices and artifacts, call forth critical responses and offer critical perspectives on extant cultural norms. Examples of such cultural critiques can be found throughout Islam, Hinduism, Buddhism, Confucianism, as well as among the animists. The dialogue between Krishna and Arjun presents an extended critical engagement with cultural imperatives. The distance between al Farabi and al Ghazali is a space filled with debate and self-examination. The popular stories of Hamza hold up common practices for examination and, occasionally, ridicule. Cultural critiques can be found in diverse sites: there is nothing about literature, philosophy, the discourses of religion, or the genres of the popular that would make these venues unable to call forth resistance.

39. Meaning is made out of difference.

There were many routes to this recognition in the twentieth century. The structuralism of Lévi-Strauss centered on it, linking linguistic structuralism to the structuralism of symbolic anthropology. Relations of difference and opposition—the relation of the raw and the cooked, hot and cold, up and down, masculine and feminine—were recognized as made meaningful in relation to one another. The proliferation of these binaries delineated the networks of meaning that constitute culture.

The recognition that meaning is made out of difference has impelled research in subaltern studies and cultural studies, and elements of critical race and feminist theories. At the simplest and often most interesting and valuable level, the delineation of oppositions serves as a tool to map culture. Charting relations of opposition enables one to map the networks of meaning that culture comprises.

Certain of these oppositions are privileged in political and cultural discourses and serve as orienting poles for identities and institutions. Civil war discourse in seventeenth-century Britain counterposed the rule of law and the rule of men, writing and blood, openness and closure. Civil war discourse in nineteenth-century America opposed slave and free, black and white, British and American, cavalier and Yankee, masculine and feminine. Egyptians have worked between the poles of the Pharoanic and the Islamic, Libyans between religious and military authority. These constitutive oppositions remind us that opposition is productive.[87] They enable us to see that oppositions are constructive: cultures and institutions are built on, around, and through them: in hybridity and fusion as well as in the play of direct opposition. This is manifest not only in the conceptual, the mythic, and the imaginary but also in the ordinary structures of practical institutional politics. Systems like party politics, for example, are built on opposition, yet research on these frequently proceeds as if opposition were a problem rather than a fundamentally unifying relation. This is also the case with regard to national and subcultural identities. In such cases, oppositions provide the orienting poles for the conceptual construction of political identity and for the movement of subjects within the networks of meaning they generate.[88]

Critics too often respond to the mapping of these relations of difference and opposition with the accusation of "binarism." This is

87. Anne Norton, *Alternative Americas* (Chicago: University of Chicago Press, 1986) and *Reflections on Political Identity*.
88. The ambivalent reference is deliberate, here and elsewhere. The networks of meaning are generated by both cultural subjects and the polar oppositions that orient their identities.

probably the result of an initial and partial recognition of the force of poststructuralist and Wittgensteinian critiques of structuralism. Although this criticism may occasionally be warranted, it more often reflects a misunderstanding of the work of difference and opposition in the creation of meaning and cultural orders. Binarisms are not invariably reductionist. Conceptually, and in linguistic and political practice, binaries are productive. Oppositions do not serve simply to limit or stabilize meaning; they proliferate meaning. Hot and cold give rise to warm and cool. Division of a political order between left and right issues in internal oppositions within each category: Montagnards and Jacobins, neo-cons and theo-cons. These binaries not only permit more precise locations for political subjects, they also produce strategic junctures at which the polarities that provide the orientation for that system may be undermined and relocated. As this suggests, oppositions are not only productive, they are dynamic. An opposition may be enduring, but within the field of meaning and orientation it creates, the terms may take on iridescence; each term can become the other. Consider an opposition with considerable mythic, literary, and historic resonance: word and flesh. The word becomes flesh (and the flesh, word) in transubstantiation and incarnation. Oppositions generate networks of meaning, strategies, and subjectivities. Accusations of binarism as simplistic may be warranted, but only if the account in question fails to delineate the dynamism and generative power of the opposition at issue.

40. Power is productive.

Power is a generative force: proliferating institutions, forms of knowledge, new subjects, and new forms of life. Once power was thought to operate only as a negative force: to forbid, to prevent, to preclude. Power not only forbids, power produces, and it produces not only institutions, laws, and regulations but also dispositions, neuroses, perversions, tastes, norms, standards, and inclinations.

Awakened by this recognition, people have learned—in politics as well as scholarship—to look for and delineate the work of power in previously ignored sites.[89] Power is seen in bio-politics: working on and in the body. Systems of knowledge, regimes of truth, and economies of desire are seen as fields of power. Subjects and institutions emerge from and within these fields: power flows in, through, from, and between them like a current. Discipline and governance, once thought of simply as regimes of constraint, become visible as systems of manufacture: factories making workers, scholars, citizens, subjects.

The recognition of power as a field, a matrix, a medium, obliges one to see power as diffuse, disseminate, and dynamic. Perhaps power was once concentrated at a single site: the king, the state. If so—and we have good reason to doubt it—it is centered no longer.[90] Power is diffused throughout the social order, operating in and on the most intimate and particular relations: on how we conceive ourselves, on the categories we employ in negotiating the world.

41. Opposition is productive.

This is not the first, and it will not be the last, thesis indebted to Hegel. Hegel's account of the dialectic is perhaps the most carefully thought out, and influential, account of the productive power of opposition. This is occasionally obscured because the dialectic is too often understood as issuing in a synthesis rather than a new opposition, and thus in a resolution. This may be the case in the last instance, but change is motivated not by resolution, but by opposi-

89. This movement in scholarship is greatly indebted to Michel Foucault, *The Order of Things: An Archaeology of the Human Sciences* (New York: Vintage, 1973), *History of Sexuality* (New York: Pantheon, 1978), *Power/Knowledge: Selected Interviews and Other Writings,* ed. Colin Gordon (New York: Pantheon 1977), and other works. Hannah Arendt did much to correct this understanding of power in the field of political theory. Theda Skocpol's *States and Social Revolution* (Cambridge: Cambridge University Press, 1979) offered a variant of this recognition, arguing that revolutions tended to increase the number and enhance the strength of state institutions.

90. Michael Hardt and Antonio Negri, *Empire* (Cambridge, Mass.: Harvard University Press, 2000). Hardt and Negri see this dissemination of power as a new phenomenon. I am more inclined to see it as a new recognition, as an old form takes a new shape.

tion. The engine of history, for Hegel, is opposition. The confrontation of two opposing forces alters each, ends the age that bore them, and propels new opposing forces into a new epoch. For Hegel, opposition produces history. Other observers, from political theory to international relations, have seen the productive power of opposition. The often contentious dialogues of Plato, in which opposing views meet, present that confrontation as productive. In a much later moment, Arendt lauded the productive power of the agon. Those who have observed the effects of enmity in international relations know that it has produced domestic change in the antagonists, spurred productions in war-related industries, and encouraged some avenues of research (witness Title 6). Comparativists (in whose company I include Americanists) have observed the productive effects of opposition in trade and manufacture. The productive effects of opposition are presumed in adversarial systems of justice, in the operation of a relatively unconstrained press, and in commitment to an electoral process.

Despite this broad recognition, in institutions and in practice, of the productive power of opposition, opposition is still too frequently portrayed as merely destructive. We are urged to aim for the resolution of conflicts—in academics and in politics. This thesis contends that this advice is misguided. We should aim not at the erasure of conflicts but at organizing and exploiting these. We should not look in scholarship for answers, resolution, and closure but for questions, debates, and the opening of new inquiries. We should not look in politics only for points of likeness and agreement, and for stability but also for the recognition and the maintenance of differences, for the fostering of debate, and, occasionally, for change, reform, and revolution.

42. Lack impels. Lack is productive.

If the former thesis could be fathered on Hegel, this might be ascribed to one of his cannibal sons, Jacques Lacan. Lacan, working from the model of the dialectic, recognized that many relations were structured around the attribution of lack and desire. One had, the other lacked; one was, the other wanted. These economies bound people together, but they were also, as Lacan observed, productive. Lack produced desire. The consciousness of want, of lack, produced the desire to remedy that lack. Lack, however, can be recognized before one knows what will remedy that lack. Hunger can be felt before the knowledge of food or of how that food is supplied. Lack can thus also be thought to produce desire in the abstract, a desire that does not know the means to its object. This desire can be fastened to objects that will not satisfy the lack but which are then recognized as desirable in their own right. Lacan has primarily been used, in the social sciences, to provide insights into the genesis and structures of identity. The motive power of lack can, however, be seen at many sites. Lack of certain necessary commodities can produce trade, or the development of substitutes, establishing or altering political relations, impelling research, encouraging industry.

An important corollary to this thesis is provided by Marx. Lack is the recognition of an unmet need, and, as Marx observed, needs can be invented. When Marx praised the ability of the bourgeoisie to invent new needs, he recognized the way in which that class had harnessed the motive power of lack. New needs produced new industries, new channels of commerce, new trade, and all that came with this vast economic expansion.

This thesis reminds the researcher (and, properly, the policymaker) that it is not only the satisfaction or the diminution of needs that should be sought but also their extension and proliferation.

43. Power comes from the absence of power.

I have given the two foregoing theses a father, and I will follow that pattern here. Ibn Khaldun, author of the *Muqaddimah,* recognized that power arose not at the center, but at the periphery.[91] Those on

91. Ibn Khaldun, *Muqaddimah,* trans. Franz Rosenthal (Princeton, N.J.: Princeton University Press, 1967). *Muqaddimah* is the Arabic word for a prologue or introduction. Ibn Khaldun's *muqaddimah,* like Hegel's, preceded a philosophic account of historical change.

the periphery, impoverished, lacking the patronage and the defenses furnished by the state to its clients, were obliged to become united and self-reliant. Lacking the resources of the state, they were obliged to look out for themselves. Having no one but themselves to rely on, they become imbued with powerful feelings—and practices—of solidarity (as Ibn Khaldun called it, *asabiyya*). There is nothing romantic about Ibn Khaldun's thesis, although it accords with a number of mythic structures. It is quite mechanical. The qualities that enable those on the periphery to take power are developed in response to the conditions they endure while out of power. These qualities of solidarity (or, as it is generally translated, group feeling) and fortitude made those on the periphery powerful, ultimately enabling them to seize the state.

Ibn Khaldun's argument also suggests that power, like interest, is not present in the abstract. Rather, there is "power to," "power for," and "power as." Power may be in relation to certain practices or certain ends and objects: the power to judge, the power to execute, the power to forgive sins. There are different types of power at work. The power to persuade differs from the power to compel by force and the power to preclude claims and questions. Power as an officer of the state or a bureaucrat, and power as a prince of the blood, belong to different regimes and neither may operate outside that regime. The appeal "I'm Arthur, your king" falls on deaf ears in the anarcho-syndicalist cooperative.[92]

44. The most effective domination is internal.

Freud's "just-so story" of the totemfeast argues for this thesis. The band of brothers, spurred by the denial of access to women, rebelled against the father's rule and thereafter divided the women among themselves. After they had killed the father and eaten him, they discovered, to their chagrin, that they were not to be free of paternal

92. *Monty Python and the Holy Grail* (1975).

rule. The father's voice now spoke from inside, and governed each of the brothers from within.[93]

Freud's myth captures important aspects of the internalization of rule. That rule which once came from outside now governs from within. That rule which was once experienced as force now operates without physical force. That rule which once came from another now comes from within oneself. Finally, and perhaps most importantly, this rule continue after the source of the rule has apparently suffered a decisive defeat.

Recognition of these features of the internalization of authority has been essential for those studying postcolonial theory, race, and sexuality. Independence did not effect the removal of those structures of subordination, deference, and exploitation that marked the colonial relation. Memmi and Mannoni, Said, Bhabha, and other postcolonial scholars have described how imperial rule is internalized and, after independence, governs the nominally independent from within.[94] Du Bois wrote of double consciousness and living behind the veil. Some of those who followed him, Henry Louis Gates, Cornel West, Anthony Appiah, bell hooks, Toni Morrison, have written of African Americans still haunted by the governing structures of racial hierarchy, structures so thoroughly inculcated that they operated not only from without but from within. Feminists recognized that sexual hierarchies operated not, for the most part, as the deliberate and willful coercion of women by men but through a set of internal norms, expectations, desires, and anxieties that made men

93. Freud, *Group Psychology and the Analysis of the Ego,* ed. and trans. James Strachey (New York: W. W. Norton, 1959). Carole Pateman gave a reading of the sexual politics of this myth and other myths of contract and covenant in *The Sexual Contract* (Stanford: Stanford University Press, 1988).

94. A number of these scholars are discussed in note 28 above. Ashis Nandy examines simultaneously psychological, rhetorical, and political efforts to overcome this internal domination throughout his work, but most notably in *The Intimate Enemy: Loss and Recovery of Self under Colonialism* (Delhi: Oxford University Press, 1983). This enterprise is chronicled in many autobiographical works, including Mohandas Karamchand Gandhi's. It is central to Nandy's enterprise, and to the reading of Gandhi in Lloyd and Susanne Rudolph, *The Modernity of Tradition.*

and women alike unconsciously complicit in the maintenance of a sexual order.

45. The most effective rule is invisible and appears as inevitable.

Those who write on hegemony in the politics of nations often refer to the predominance—especially the military or economic predominance—of a single state. The United States in the late twentieth century appears in this hegemonic role. In this form, hegemony is grand, conspicuous, brandishing very large weapons that—if hegemony prevails—will be little used. Power in this form is interrupted, uneven, and uncertain.

There are other forms of hegemony, less evident, more effective, and more pervasive. These are neither grand nor conspicuous. Imperial powers learned, in the eighteenth and nineteenth centuries (if not much earlier) that the maintenance of power depends not on what can be seen, but on what need not show itself. Imperial rule is best secured not by obedience to armed men, but by habits of deference. As independence removed the grand and the conspicuous from imperial power, the working of these habits of deference—in practice, in habit, in thought, in assumptions, in the construction of desire—could be more easily discerned. Older theorists of hegemony were read again, and people learned to look for those forms of power that rely on an invisible ubiquity.[95] Gramsci and those who followed him recognized that the capacity of rule to call forth resistance was diminished when and where the rule appeared as inevitable, and outside politics.

These hegemonic structures govern thought and the categories of thought, desire, and the designation of objects of desire. They often

95. Most of the discussion of this form of rule appear in the literature on hegemony that moves from Gramsci to Raymond Williams, Stuart Hall, and Slavoj Zizek. Antonio Gramsci, *Selections from the Prison Notebooks,* ed. and trans. Quintin Hoare (New York: International Publishers, 1971); Raymond Williams, *The Raymond Williams Reader,* ed. John Higgins (London: Blackwell, 2001); Judith Butler, Ernesto Laclau, Slavoj Zizek, *Contingency, Hegemony, Universality* (London: Verso, 2000).

appear in the guise of the natural, that which is understood as given, prior to politics, and inalterable. They work as assumptions: what anyone would want, what no one would want, what we can take for granted. The taken for granted, the given, the commonplace, and other silences operate as negative space in a composition. They may initially appear as unused or neglected space, but a more careful examination reveals that they contribute to the composition as fully as filled spaces. Recognizing this, one learns to look for power in the practices and structures governing political subjects in their daily lives. Questioning the taken for granted fulfills the ethical imperative identified by Weber "to ask questions about those things that convention makes self-evident"[96] and the older imperative "the unexamined life is not worth living."

Many things once taken for granted have come into question in the past century, the notions, for example, that race is physical and biological, that masculinity and femininity are natural, that power has a center and that center is the state, that dreams are mere illusions, without meaning. Once these were no longer taken for granted, entire fields of inquiry opened, new disciplines emerged. If we soon found we were taking other things for granted, we had nevertheless uncovered certain suspect old certainties and accustomed ourselves to regarding the new ones as potential prey.

The most powerful—and the most commonplace—forms of hegemony are to be found in language. It is in language that the discreet, or unobserved, construction of what we take for granted, what we feel we must want, and what we cannot refuse to desire is most fully accomplished. These conventional desires appear to us not as impositions but as natural and inevitable. They appear to us as our own.

46. Domination is through and of the senses.

Domination is not a formal relation, nor an abstract concept. Domination is intimate, working not only upon peoples but on men and

---

96. Weber, *The Methodology of the Social Sciences*, 13.

women. That work is done not only on battlefields and courts of law but in the factory, the shop, and the servants' quarters, in the fields and in the bedroom. Domination is material, working through the construction of roads and aqueducts, the provision of electricity and irrigation, the architecture of prison, factory, and school. Domination is sensual.

The senses provide practical guidance to the study of domination in its most magnificent and most intimate forms. Taken one by one, they reveal modes and avenues of domination that are too often neglected by scholars. Sight is the sense most recognized as a mode of domination. Studies of veiling, although they have often been invidious and misleading, have nevertheless led scholars to recognize the operation of an economy of sight, and the work that economy does in the subjection—and liberation—of women. Whether one regards the veil as removing women from the public sphere or permitting them to enter it, constructing them as wholly sexual beings, or removing them from the discourse of sexuality, one is obliged to recognize the controversy over veiling as an instance of politics on the plane of sight.[97] This line of research has perhaps been very effectively pursued in colonial and postcolonial studies. Roland Barthes's reading of a photograph of a black soldier saluting the French tricolor is one of the iconic episodes in the history of semiotics. Malek Alloula saw how erotic (or, more accurately, obscene) French postcards of colonized women made visible the interrelation of sexual and colonial dominion and eroticized the colonial relation.[98] Colonial photography gave otherwise untraveled and often impoverished imperial subjects access to the visual pleasure of possession and domination. A Yorkshire miner or a Manchester tradesman could enjoy seeing all the monuments of a vast empire and was given access as well to the most intimate spaces of the colonized: their temples, their homes, their bodies. Photography, painting, and

97. Particularly good studies of veiling have been done by Nilufer Gole, in *The Forbidden Modern* (Ann Arbor: University of Michigan Press, 1996), and by Elizabeth Warnock Fernea, in her documentary *Veiled Revolution.*

98. Malek Alloula, *The Colonial Harem,* trans. Myrna Godzich and Wlad Godzich (Minneapolis: University of Minnesota Press, 1986).

other visual representations of empire extended participation in and enjoyment of imperial dominion and gathered political support for often costly and illegitimate imperial enterprises. Questions concerning who and what is seen, what must be seen, what cannot be seen, who is able to see, and who is denied access to these sights open up vast fields of inquiry and make otherwise concealed relations visible.[99]

Each of the senses serves as a field and instrument of domination. The ear, as Lacan remarked, is "the only orifice that cannot be closed." Sound is thus a particularly apt tool of domination. The extent of Islam can be heard in the call to prayer, the extent of Anglo-American power in the sounds of English. Silence is death, AIDS activists argue. In other contexts, at other moments, silence protects and privileges. Taste and smell—the taste of the host, the smell of incense—give access to the boundaries of cultural communities and their norms. They also open the operation of economic power to us. What people eat, where they shit, whether they have water, whether they can be clean, are questions that bring domination home.

47. Prohibitions produce institutions and resistances. Prohibitions interpellate identities.

This thesis takes up another of the lines of thought that runs through theses 42, 43, 44, and 45, bringing it to identities and institutions, to the material and the particular. These theses explore the productive power of negation. Earlier theses delineated different modes and sites of interpellation. Here these two concerns meet. Nietzsche wrote of how a few "thou shalt nots," with their attendant punishments, could create "a being with the right to make promises." Foucault wrote of how the categorization and prohibition of departures from the normal created sexual pathologies and medical and legal institutions responding to them. The identification of these perver-

99. Anne Norton, *Bloodrites of the Poststructuralists* (New York: Routledge, 2002).

sities, inversions, diseases, or preferences (according to the time and place) created identities: gays, pedophiles, foot fetishists, lesbians, nymphomaniacs. Similarly, the identification of any medical syndrome creates specializations and experts, and often research and charitable organizations. The identification of a practice as criminal may bring that practice into being or expand its use and will create corresponding institutions in law and scholarship. This phenomenon has long been recognized in practice, by legislators who hesitated to enumerate crimes (particularly crimes of vice) for fear of enticing the already criminal and corrupting the innocent.

48. Ruling structures constrain the rulers as well as the ruled, the advantaged as well as the disadvantaged.

Does advantage betray intention? Arrangements that advantage a class are often assumed to be the conscious and deliberate work of that class. This assumption is often in error and nearly always misleading. The temptation to the error is very great. It gives someone to blame and it suggests that those who are to blame can change the system. If you are privileged unjustly, you can disavow that privilege. Thus white people of good (or, more precisely, bad) conscience are urged to become "race traitors." Albert Memmi knew better. Memmi wrote of the problem of "the good colonizer" who recognizes the unearned privileges he receives under the colonial system and refuses them. However he tries, Memmi wrote, he will be unable to disavow these; the privileges will be given to him whether he wants them or not. His only recourse is to escape the systems and the structures that privilege him.[100]

Structures are not simply responsive to the intentions of those they advantage, at least not as particular people. First, not all of the advantaged are immediately apparent. Institutions may serve the interests of classes other than those they obviously advantage. Imperial

100. Albert Memmi, *The Coloniser and the Colonised*, 19–44.

structures, for example, served not only the interests of expatriate colonizers but also those of the regime, particular political parties, mercantile and religious interests. Second, although structures may be put in place in the first instance by members of a particular class with deliberation and specific intentions, they acquire distinct institutional interests that may become wholly or partially autonomous from the intentions of their authors. They have unexpected consequences and acquire unintended powers.

The case becomes more interesting with hegemonic ruling structures. These structures, which manifest themselves in what is taken for granted, what cannot be questioned, in what appears natural and given, are the most powerfully constraining and they operate on the rulers as well as the ruled. Consider issues of sexuality. Patriarchal structures, or other arrangements that favor men over women, nevertheless constrain men. Men are obliged to accord to certain highly constrained models of masculine identity and are given a set of duties and obligations as well as privileges. Where heterosexuality is privileged similar constraints apply. Heterosexuals are privileged, but they are by no means unconstrained. They are subject to prohibitions and imperatives that define their privileged status. They are called to behave in certain ways and punished for deviations.

49. That which is overcome, remains.

Defeat is essential to politics. In politics, some win, some lose; some causes prosper, some fade. Victory and defeat overcome movements. In victory a movement overcomes both its opponent and itself, becoming an institution or becoming part of those conventions that are taken for granted. Defeat may overcome a movement in another, more ordinary sense, causing it to disappear from the political landscape. Societies have occupations and identities, institutions, practices, languages, and rituals that seem to fall victim to the effects of time and altered conditions. This thesis contends that these, though overcome, remain. They remain in record and memory. Because that which preserves the past is in the present, that which is past remains in the present. The past is present as that which once was, and might be again; or as that which was not, but might have been. That which was once defeated remains to present alternatives, however distant and improbable, that can be taken up again in an altered form. Defeated movements remain because they have been overcome. That which defeated them preserves them, for the memory of the victory and the identity of the victor depend on that which was overcome.

50. Nothing runs ahead of its time. Many things run ahead of their time.

Marx's claim that nothing runs ahead of its time corrects naïve conceptions of a vanguard, or a "great man" who comes to us as the emissary of a future, and of revolutions or reforms that propel a reluctant or unsuspecting present into the future. The present is the site of our presence. Past and future are present to us only there, only in the present. Forces, even the forces of change, do not appear de novo but emerge from and in relation to particular cultural configurations: institutions, social structures, and other conditions, systems, and forces.

Yet in another sense many things run ahead of their time. The meaning of a person or an act, a word or an event is not exhausted in the moment of its enactment or utterance. These things exceed the initial site where they take place. Constitutions, anticolonial manifestos, and nationalist narratives create imagined countries and citizens that the living struggle to create. Legislation, regulations, prescriptive and proscriptive policies influence the policies, practices, and behavior that follows them. The work of politics is undertaken not for the present alone but for a future into which the living and the dead extend their will. This work exceeds them, having effects they neither intended nor foresaw. In all these respects, things run ahead of their time.

51. Facts do not speak for themselves.

Facts do not speak for themselves. Facts speak for the value and utility of particular methods. Facts speak for the authors who marshal
them in speeches, documents and depositions, scholarly articles, and
popular polemics. Facts speak within a political context, where they
may serve to protect some and endanger others.

Max Weber reserved particular scorn for the strategy of "letting
the facts speak for themselves." This was, he observed, a favored
rhetorical device in parliamentary speeches, and "quite legitimately,
given their purposes." For scholars, the pretense of letting the facts
speak for themselves, is "of all abuses, the most abhorrent."[101]

Weber aimed his criticism at the guile that sought to disguise eval-
uation in a nominally neutral presentation. Evaluative judgments
are always already present in facts. Facts are made. Facts are artifacts,
produced by particular research methods. Facts are constructed, or
if you prefer, chosen to appear in a particular analytic narrative.
They are marshaled by a researcher, for a particular purpose. They
appear in the narrative in the rhetorical service of that argumenta-
tive purpose. This is acknowledged most explicitly in the judicial
system where findings of fact are understood not as "what happened" in the ordinary language sense but in relation to the conventions of law and adjudication. The choice of which facts will
appear in an analysis is governed by local disciplinary conventions
and (let us not forget) may be influenced, if not determined, by political considerations.

52. Facts are made.

Fact derives from the Latin *factum,* a thing done.[102] Facts are done,
made. Scholars, even those who represent themselves as "discover-

---

101. Weber, *The Methodology of the Social Sciences,* 10.
102. *Compact Edition of the Oxford English Dictionary,* vol. 1 (London:
Oxford University Press, 1984), 947. "We are all philologists now," Nietzsche
writes in *On the Genealogy of Morals.*

ing" facts, know that facts are the result of work. Whether this process is seen as "digging" or "assembly," "sifting through material," or "collating data," "mining," or "diving for pearls," it is acknowledged as a form of labor, a making. Those facts that appear to be the matter of history are themselves constructs, the work of the historian.[103] Facts come into being in language. Those material circumstances to which they refer, or from which they are derived, are not exhausted by the name, phrase, or description that purports to capture them. They belong to the inexhaustible particular.

With an eye (or a wink) to scholarly future, one might also advance the multivocal and polemical, but no less accurate, reading: "facts are done."

53. Facts are artifacts of the methods that produce them.

This thesis mirrors an observation made by King, Keohane, and Verba: "The content is the method." Though they cited the principle, they failed to fully recognize its implications. King, Keohane, and Verba wrote that "scientific research adheres to a set of rules of inference on which its validity depends." (This is a local instance of what Foucault called a "truth regime.") Science refers not to objects of study or to results of research but to these rules alone. They quote approvingly from a nineteenth-century paean, "The field of science is unlimited; its material is endless; every group of natural phenomena, every phase of social life, every stage of past or present development is material for science. The unity of all science consists alone in its method, not in its material."[104] Science figures here as a universal tool that can be brought to bear on any material. The tool is of human construction, the material outside and independent of it. Yet a simple reading of the passage demonstrates that it is quite the other way. The material on which science works has already been

---

103. Michael Oakeshott, "Historical Experience" in *Experience and Its Modes* (Cambridge: Cambridge University Press, 1995), 86–168.

104. King et al., *Designing Social Inquiry,* 9.

named, sorted, and characterized by it. The ostensibly given material has already been shaped by science. The field on which science works has already been divided into the natural and the social, and it has already been made historical. Science is always allied to its objects. Though these objects are indeed unlimited, they are not separable from the scientific enterprise.

54. There are no neutral methods.

Methods, like subjects, are formed within culture. They bear the marks of that culture. Meaning is constructed within networks that have linguistic and political dimensions. Meaningful action occurs within, and with reference to, these networks. Methods are dependent on the always limited and parochial systems of reference within these networks in order to figure as meaningful action and to produce meaningful work. Methods are allied with particular regimes of truth.

Methods are governed by assumptions. Rational choice methods assume a rational subject, operating with (usually more than relative) autonomy. They produce explanations consistent with the rationality they presuppose. Realist explanations in the study of international relations assume the state, a state capable of acting as an agent, in a state system, and motivated by an unwavering and consistent commitment to survival and relative power. Marxists assume the priority of the economic, hermeneuticists the presence of meaning. The assumptions a given method makes may be warranted, they may be correct, but they are not neutral.

Methods are devised and employed in institutions. Those institutions are part of a political economy. They may be funded by private donations, corporate subsidies, private or public endowments, public research funds, and a variety of other means. Which methods are developed, and which employed, are directly linked to these sources of funding. When the Ford Foundation or the Social Science Research Council decides to discourage area studies or encourage multicountry studies, it is explicitly promulgating a research agenda and attempting to influence the research agendas of the scholars that organization funds. Such efforts may be legitimate interventions in the work of the academy, but they run counter to methodological neutrality at the institutional level. Such efforts are successful only when individuals respond to monetary incentives in choosing the questions they ask, the topics they study, and the methods they employ.

The forces that work against methodological neutrality are diverse. They range from deliberate attempts to politicize research to the often subtle and unintended effects of differential funding, from institutional systems of incentives to the ethical and political imperatives of the researcher. Researchers are impelled by ideal as well as material motives: they are moved by considerations of duty as well as advantage.

55. There are no neutral scientists.

Scholars, scientists, and students are subjects formed, like other subjects, in culture. They are, in this cultural context, ascribed sex, race, and age. They are located within networks of meaning that determine their class and regional identities, and determine the requirements of their occupations. They are within language, within culture, within politics. Each has a specific location and a particular set of perspectives that follow from that location. All are partial, in both senses. This partiality, and the particularities of each perspective, make certain phenomena available for observation and exclude others. This is the vantage point of place. These are the limits of place. At these sites are found the duties, the drives, and the passions of place: of politics, history, religion, friendship, and kinship.

Scholars, scientists, and students are bound within a complex of constraints and desires, needs and obligations. The necessity of earning a living, the desirability of earning regard, make certain lines of research advantageous and attractive and foreclose others. There are limits and vantage points at these sites as well. The need to see, to learn, to teach, to make the silent heard, the hidden seen is a drive and an obligation, a duty and a passion.

How then should we consider the old ideal of ethical neutrality? When Weber wrote on ethical neutrality, professors spoke "in governmentally privileged lecture halls, where they are neither controlled, checked by discussion, or subject to contradiction."[105] Conditions are different now and we are safer for it. We are not, however, protected from the constraints that states and institutions, popular prejudice and academic privilege impose on teaching, writing, and research. We must be conscious of those constraining—and inciting—structures. We must recognize, where we can, the taken for granted, and the other imperatives that govern speech in silence. We must recognize that even where all can speak not all can be heard, that some speech panders and other speech takes courage, and that the courageous are not always the correct.

56. Work speaks simultaneously of its ostensible object and of its author and context.

The recognition that no research, and no researcher, is neutral is often received with frustration as a form of debunking with paralyzing results. That results from the mistaken belief that partiality renders work useless or illegitimate. Those who have read the Federalist Papers, Marx, or any number of other valuable polemical works should have been inoculated against this assumption. Partiality or, in the term favored by Burke, prejudice does not necessarily diminish a work's value in illuminating its object. Familiarity, experience, and affection limit what one sees, but they also open what might remain concealed or unnoticed. The passions that drive

---

105. It is frequently assumed that Weber, in his famous essay "The Meaning of Ethical Neutrality," argued that "the assertion of value judgments should be held to a minimum," a position that Weber explicitly characterizes as "untenable." Weber, *The Methodology of the Social Sciences*.

polemics drive investigation and arguments as well. There are reliable and unreliable polemics. If one considers a work as not only bearing on an object of study but as an object of study in its own right, one recognizes that partiality can serve as a source of knowledge, rather than an impediment to it.

As is so often the case, I practiced this unconsciously and learned it only when challenged. A reviewer reproached me for referring to a book review of Bancroft's *History of the United States* rather than to the work itself. I was writing of southern identity in the antebellum period. The review (in the *Southern Literary Messenger*) spoke of that identity in detail and offered an indictment of Bancroft's conception of the South and the place of the South in the United States. Reading Bancroft would not have provided evidence for southern conceptions of southern identity. The review, written by a southerner for a southern audience on the subject of a peculiarly southern identity, did. My critic erred in assuming that a given work is either a "primary" or a "secondary" source and remains in that category whatever the context. It is not the work but the relation of the work to the question at hand that determines the type and value of the evidence it furnishes.

Because a work speaks simultaneously of its ostensible object and its author and context, a work may be of great value to a researcher even if it is full of error or a tissue of lies. Look at two particularly notorious examples: D. W. Griffiths's films *Birth of a Nation* and *The Protocols of the Elders of Zion*. Insofar as these works speak of their ostensible objects, they lie. Yet they make visible forms of domination, systems of oppression, and discourses of subjection that might otherwise go unseen or denied. *The Protocols of the Elders of Zion* is not a reliable source of evidence on international relations or the history of the Jews. It is, however, an invaluable source of evidence on the character and discourses of antisemitism; on the traits ascribed to Jews, the fictive histories in which they were embedded, and the complex of anxieties, enmities, and resentments of antisemites. *Birth of a Nation* is not a reliable account of the birth of any nation, or of the Reconstruction and "Redemption" it purports to chronicle. Yet it provides insight not only into the mythology of the Klu Klux Klan but also into the interweaving of race and sex in American racism.[106] It would be foolish to assume that the best evidence can be obtained from the most objective sources. The best evidence on instances of demonization, on racism, on religious belief, and on revolutionary passion can often be obtained from the least objective sources: the sources that express or exemplify them.

Cultural work, or indeed any work at all, can (and should) be read in several ways. It may be read as an account of its subject, or it may be taken as an artifact in its own right. It may be read as a work on a particular subject, as a work of its time, or as a work of its author. Each work is thus capable of furnishing evidence to, and shedding light upon, an array of radically different questions and intellectual projects.

57. There are no general laws.

The conviction that research in the social sciences might result in the discovery of general laws analogous to the law of gravity in Newtonian physics is the residue of the effort to make research in the social sciences accord to a model derived from the seventeenth-century natural sciences. Ironically, the derivative discourses of scientific investigation in the social sciences have adhered to a crude understanding of "general laws" as the "hard sciences" from which they nominally took their bearings qualified and refined it.

Laws, like other artifacts of method, issue from culturally particular modes of investigation, and culturally particular regimes of truth. These laws are commonly produced within institutions and ratified by them. They are determined in part by the availability and division of research funds, and the constraints placed on research by

106. This is demonstrated in Michael Rogin's brilliant reading of the film in *Ronald Reagan: The Movie and Other Episodes in Political Demonology* (Berkeley: University of California Press, 1987).

the state, religion, private funding agencies, social practices, and ethical norms. They are the result of particular modes of investigation, the artifacts of the methods that produced them.

When confronted with "general laws," one ought to subject the claim to a double critique. First, one can examine the claim to universality. Second, one can explore the cultural structures, institutions, and methodological systems that produced the research advancing the claim.

58. There is no evidence. Evidence is always of and for something.

The object of this thesis is to ensure that claims to have evidence, or challenges to evidence, are always attended by certain basic and absolutely fundamental questions. Evidence for what? Evidence of what? Evidence for whom? The answers to these questions determine the type of evidence required, the sources that might provide it, and the value to be attached to it.

Economic interpretations assume an economic explanation and look for economic evidence. What counts as evidence is determined by the governing interpretation.[107] One looks *at* economic data. One looks *for* instances where economic forces appear determinative. When one finds such instances, one has found evidence. One is not expected, much less required, to look at other types of data, or to look for instances where economic forces are not determinative. The evidence is, in a very practical sense, interpellated—called for—by the theory assumed and the methods employed.

The practices of the investigator, although—or rather, because—they adhere scrupulously to conventional standards of scholarly

---

107. Stanley Fish, in an early and influential article on this point, wrote, "the interpretation determines what will count as evidence for it, and the evidence is able to be picked out only because the interpretation has *already* been assumed" (Stanley Fish, "Normal Circumstances, Literal Language, Direct Speech Acts, the Ordinary, the Everyday, the Obvious, What Goes Without Saying, and Other Special Cases," in Rabinow and Sullivan, eds., *Interpretive Social Science: A Reader*).

rigor, call up the evidence they look for. This does not mean that investigators always find the evidence they desire. That evidence may run counter to the particular claims made. The researcher may find that there is no evidence to support the claim, or that the evidence found supports another argument. The evidence will however, remain within the field defined by theory and method. The presence of evidence for one argument or explanation does not, therefore, foreclose the possibility that there is evidence—as much and as good—for another.

This alone should ensure that no explanation, however powerful, is taken to exclude all others.

59. Nothing is noncontributory.

A more immediately accessible wording of this thesis might be: Nothing is necessarily noncontributory. This version reminds the researcher that few decisions on salience can be rendered in advance. Those who work in archives or in the field tend to learn this rapidly. I was once in Delhi to research the nationalism of Maharajah Jai Singh of Alwar in the National Archives. While buying sensible books in a bookshop, I came across (in addition to Khushwant Singh's jokebook) a set of used comic books on the Indian Mutiny. I bought these because of an earlier interest in popular culture, a liking for kitsch, and the thought that I could use the illustrations from The Rani of Jhansi in a mixed-media composition. Instead I found an invaluable alternative history of the Indian independence movement, and a text that gave me access to the political import of the tiger preserve that Jai Singh had established at Sariska. Virtually every researcher has had experiences of this sort. Such an experience can not be laid to mere serendipity or good research karma. Instead it should be recognized as an index of the inexhaustible complex of references available in any cultural artifact. Each artifact gives access to systems of circulation, political economies, economies of desire, multiple discourses, literary and historical references, and a host of other avenues of inquiry.

This version has as its (chastening) corollary: Most things are non-contributory to any given analysis. Researchers are obliged, by theory and experience, to acknowledge that we are not always positioned to exploit that which is made available in a given artifact. We are conscious of the vast amount of material we have found that proved if not irrelevant, at least impenetrable. We know, and we commonly regret, the avenues that a lack of time or skill, or political constraints, prevented us from exploring, even in the material we used. One might say that while nothing is necessarily noncontributory in principle, in effect, most things are not contributory. This furnishes a continuing reminder of the limits of our apprehension and our research.

60. That which is omitted, absent, and silent is as important as that which is committed, present, and conspicuous.

This thesis is an exhortation to research in negative space. Work on hegemony requires the recognition not only of what must be said but also of what cannot be said and what cannot be asked. Work on the subaltern requires the capacity, the commitment, and the skills to recognize a presence in an absence. This is no precious or arcane formula but a simple description of the demands placed on those who study the undocumented and the inadequately documented. In the course of research, the undocumented must become the indirectly and obliquely documented. Their presence will be made visible by inference and implication, by recognizing what is omitted in a text, presupposed in a relation, made necessary by an institution. The radicalism of that effort was revealed in Gayatri Spivak's still daunting essay "Can the Subaltern Speak?" The answer was not the utopian "yes" but a "no" that demanded recognition of the full intellectual and political effects of enforced silence.[108]

108. Gayatri Chakravorty Spivak, "Can the Subaltern Speak?" in *The Postcolonial Studies Reader,* ed. Bill Ashcroft, Gareth Griffiths, Helen Tiffin (New York: Routledge, 1995), 24–28.

Works written under political scrutiny or under the reign—popular or authoritarian—of religious dogmas often have passages written in the negative space. A quotation may be not quite finished, and that which precedes or follows it may carry a trenchant critique that cannot be written but can be carried in spaces within the text. The texts of rebellion and resistance are more often written in hidden transcripts than in *cahiers de doleances.*

61. Description entails analysis.

Theodore Lowi is said to have declared to a class in the declamatory tones of Texas oratory, "Describe, describe, describe, and you have *explained* it!" Lowi's statement is not merely right, it is right in more than one way. There is, as many inspired readers of ethnographies have observed, no description without analysis. The decision about *what* to describe entails the recognition and selection of definitive events, practices, or attributes. The decision about *how* to describe identifies those aspects of the events, practices, or attributes that determine their relevance to the analysis. The researcher who describes a Balinese cockfight, for example, has determined that the cockfight is revelatory. The description of that practice makes a covert argument for the cultural importance of that practice. The description of betting on the cockfight embeds the practice in an economic order. The decision to describe a given process as fast or slow acknowledges or establishes a normal rate and marks rate (rate of growth, rate of expansion) as a constitutive, and important, dimension of the process concerned.

Lowi's exhortation can be read, however, as making a more thorough-going argument for description. The particular testifies always and only to itself. The imperative to describe acknowledges the importance of the particular. It is not enough, this exhortation insists, to identify a supposedly determinative factor. One must continue to describe if one is to explain.

Finally, the repeated exhortation to "describe, describe, describe" suggests the inexhaustibility of the particular. Though one describes endlessly, though one returns again and again to the phenomenon, one cannot exhaust it. In this reading, the exhortation "describe, describe, and you have *explained* it" mocks the claim to give a final or exhaustive explanation.[109]

62. No account can be comprehensive.

Once, and perhaps still in certain circles, one was taught to aspire to writing a "comprehensive" or "definitive" history. This ambition assumed a linear view of history, an assumption that permitted a writer arriving later on the scene to assume that with sufficient diligence (and, perhaps, a degree of assistance from the Fates who keep the necessary documents from destruction) he could see the past whole. He had, by virtue of his place in time, a view of what lay behind him. It might be necessary to uncover or to remove obstructions, but in principle the historical lay behind him, never to be altered. What one found of the past was unaltered and inalterable. The form and content of the past were set, and because they were set, the historian could give an account of that past that would be complete, never requiring additions or alterations. This aspiration was, however, not one that could be accomplished.

The most accessible set of objections is the practical, or empirical, one. People die, documents are destroyed, artifacts decay. What remains of the past is materially partial, in every sense. It is only part of what once existed. Time may favor those whose objects were better built, out of stronger materials, or being more valuable were

---

109. When he first commented on these theses, William Sewell observed that a number were, and more could be, inverted. This is one of those that might be doubled. Description entails analysis. Analysis entails description. The designation of parts and the articulation of relations between them entails description, of those parts and of the manner of their articulation. The analysis informs our understanding of the categories, providing, obliquely, descriptions of their constitutive attributes.

more carefully preserved. Time favors the wealthy and the powerful. Time favors those who kept records, kept those records in order,
in places and materials that would preserve them. Time favors those
who write about themselves, publish those writings, and disseminate them broadly. Time favors the literate and the bureaucratic, the
commercial and the imperial. Those who had access to records
might cull those they did not wish to survive. The materials of the
past are incomplete in the present, and the historian, however dili-
gent, who works with incomplete materials, can furnish no more
than an incomplete account. These are, however, not the most powerful obstacles to offering a definitive or comprehensive account of
the past.

The sense that time, and consequently meaning, events, and ourselves, moves inexorably forward belongs not to events but to ourselves.[110] It is an artifact of our understanding. The belief in the linearity of time that undergirds ambitions to construct comprehensive
or definitive histories is undercut by this recognition.

The past constitutes the present but the present also constitutes
the past. Each successive moment sees the past from a different vantage point, invests the past with a meaning that refers to itself, and
experiences new aspects of that which the past leaves behind and
before it. It is not merely accounts of the past that are altered in the
present and in the future. The past is not sealed unaltered and inalterable in time. Institutions, and other structures, grow in anticipated and in unanticipated directions, and as they do, the past takes
fuller form in the present. The prison shows itself not simply as a
means of more humane punishment but as the inauguration of a
new set of strategies for the exercise of power.[111] History does not
simply move forward. It constantly turns and doubles back upon itself, returning to alter some point from which it came, taking that
point to its center once again, enfolding it in subsequent events.

110. Immanuel Kant, *Critique of Pure Reason,* trans. Norman Kemp Smith
(New York: St. Martin's Press, 1965), section II, 6a, 77. This is discussed more
extensively in thesis 83.

111. Michel Foucault, *Discipline and Punish.*

The aspiration to furnishing comprehensive or definitive accounts was not confined to historians. Those who studied institutions, or other nominally discrete phenomena, might also pretend to offer complete accounts of those phenomena. These too are inadequate before the temporal range of the objects. As an institution continues in and over time it reveals previously unrecognized and unrealized aspects of itself. As these aspects come into being they alter the institution not only as it is but as it was and will be.[112]

63. Representation alters the represented.

This thesis has, as so many do, a deliberate multivocality and speaks to both politics and scholarship.

In politics, as a political institution, representation has long been recognized, lauded, and deprecated for its constitutive effects. Those who praised it argued that representation refined the views of the represented. The represented chose representatives more intelligent, more learned, more restrained, more disciplined, and more committed than themselves. These representatives refined the opinions of the people, tamed their passions, directed their wills and their appetites to appropriate objects. They were not mere channels for transmission. They were to represent the people, the people's will, as the people wished it to be: to will as the people would will if they had the capacities of their chosen representatives. Their actions informed the people of what their character and their will should be, and the people, thus informed, altered themselves accordingly. Another praise of representation commended it for its efficiency, and for removing the burdens of governance from the majority of the people. In this view, representation freed people to pursue their private, self-chosen ends. Both views of representation recognized that representation changed the represented: both the represented constituencies, and their represented wills.

112. T. S. Eliot, "Burnt Norton," in *Four Quartets* (New York: Harcourt Brace, 1943).

Those who suspected or condemned representative political institutions also recognized the constitutive effects of representation. They argued that the representatives translated the opinions of the people into a warrant for the representatives' personal advancement, that representation made public judgment and public will partial, that representation transformed political actors into domesticated subjects, that it accustomed people to indifference and apathy. These arguments too recognized that representation altered the represented.

Given this commonplace recognition of the constitutive effects of representation in politics, resistance to the recognition of the effects of representation in the study of politics seems disingenuous. The effects of representation appear as clearly in the study of politics as they do in politics itself. The claim of the scholar for scholarship echoes the partisans of representation. The anthropologist claims to bring the Samoans or the Nambikwara before you. The historian's work claims that if you had the necessary languages, read the archives, and knew the context, then you would see the history as the work presents it. The survey researcher claims that if you asked all the people in America, the opinions expressed would be the same as those represented by the random sample. Lacking the time or the capacity, or the plane tickets, one can rely on the resources of others. Lacking knowledge and the means to acquire it, one can learn through the labor of others. We know that these representations (some more than others) alter the public world. We know that Burke's French may be British and Tocqueville's Americans may be French, that the Islam we learn may be Hourani's or Huntington's. We know that a reliance on expertise may replace independent inquiry, that reputation may stand in the place of research. We know that the representation alters the represented.

One could go much further. One could ask, as Lévi-Strauss and Derrida did, what writing represented among the Nambikwara.[113]

113. Derrida, *Of Grammatology.*

64. Quantification is distortion.

Quantification is, at bottom, a system of representation, and like all systems of representations, it alters the represented. I have termed that representation a distortion here to counter the claims of precision and scientific neutrality so blindly (or shamelessly) forwarded by its practitioners. This thesis will take up three distortions effected by quantitative social science: distortions in the understanding of method, distortions in the teaching of method, and distortions in the representation and analysis of data. These are exemplary, not exhaustive.

In political science and sociology, practitioners of quantitative social science have divided the world in two: the quantitative and the "qualitative" and (coincident with these) the "hard and the soft." The rubric "qualitative methods" testifies to certain fundamental defects in this understanding. The methods conflated under this rubric differ dramatically in their analytic approaches and intellectual antecedents. "Qualitative analysis" includes, for example, Marxist political economists, Straussian exegetes, positivists, and poststructuralists. The implication that "qualitative methods" do not employ quantitative data or techniques is absurd, but the absurdity is concealed by this misleading dichotomy. In a display of the enduring power of the concept of false consciousness, this distinction has been accepted by many, among them King, Keohane, and Verba. The dichotomy reserves to quantitative social science the prestige attached to the numbers as a form of representation.

The dichotomy of "hard" and "soft" ascribes precision and rigor to quantitative social science largely on the basis of the deployment of systems of numerical representation and their use of mathematical techniques. This curious faith in numbers is remarkable when one observes that much quantification is effected by the arbitrary assignment of subjectively determined values, or the rough translation of an adjective into a numerical form. Consider the following examples. A content analysis counts the occurrence of references to slavery. This does not include literary allusions or references that do not employ the term *slave*. If such an analysis were made of the American Constitution, the analyst would conclude that this document took no notice of slavery. Subjects are queried on their responses to a set of questions after having been primed by reading articles that have been "gendered" by the experimenter. The "gendering" consists in the experimenter inserting into the article expressions of opinions on hierarchy and the givenness of social roles, sentiments he believes represent prevailing views on gender. What is measured is accordance to the researcher's imaginary, no more. In such instances, which are ubiquitous in survey research, quantification lends only the pretense of precision and rigor.

Measurement might be thought to be a more rigorous version of quantification. While quantification may be (particularly in practice) entirely subjective, measurement requires the application of extant tools, techniques, and quantifying systems. The politics of measurement have been described, and critiqued, extensively throughout the social sciences and the humanities. Sociologists, anthropologists, historians, and literary critics have described the invidious effects of particular enterprises of measurement undertaken by orientalist scholars, imperial civil servants, and colonial administrators.[114] Wittgenstein observed the same phenomenon: "The Jew is always measured on scales which do not fit him."[115] Feminists have detailed the manipulation of standards of measurement and assessment as artifacts of, and insurance for, the preservation of systems privileging men.[116] Measurement is within culture, within politics. The close institutional ties and structures of mutual dependence and

114. Michael Adas, *Machines as the Measure of Men: Science, Technology, and Ideologies of Western Dominance* (Ithaca: Cornell University Press, 1989). See also Sander Gilman, *Difference and Pathology: Stereotypes of Sexuality, Race, and Madness* (Ithaca: Cornell University Press, 1985).

115. Wittgenstein, *Culture and Value*, 16e.

116. An early and still influential example was Catherine MacKinnon, *Feminism Unmodified* (Cambridge, Mass.: Harvard University Press, 1987). See also *Sex and Scientific Inquiry*, ed. Sandra Harding and Jean F. O'Barr (Chicago: University of Chicago Press, 1987).

advantage that link political, economic, and scientific institutions suggest that measurement should be regarded not as relatively neutral, but as particularly suspect.

The effects of distortion through translation and representation are not limited to quantitative social science. I take up the distortions of formality in the thesis that follows. Quantitative social science does however bear intellectual and ethical responsibility for the distortions that have characterized the teaching of methods in the American social sciences.

Courses in "methodology" and "research methods" in political science are commonly limited to the teaching of quantitative methods: statistics and, in some cases, rational choice, game theory, and formal modeling. The syllabi and the texts used in such courses exclude political theory outright. Thus students are not exposed to methods employed in the field of political theory: analytic philosophy, logic, hermeneutics, semiotics, and other interpretive techniques. Students acquire a similarly truncated view of comparative and American politics, lacking exposure to the historical methods undergirding the study of American political development, the methods of legal research and interpretation central to the study of public law and constitutional theory, the ethnographic methods employed in urban politics and comparative politics, and instruction in the practice and ethics of fieldwork. This is despite the fact that these methods have been carefully and rigorously articulated, frequently critiqued and defended, and consistently taught in other disciplines. This is a multiple deprivation: students whose work demands these methods are left to fend for themselves, while students not employing them understand all but quantitative methods as informal enterprises, lacking in rigor. Occasionally, exposure to "qualitative methods" is tacked on as an addendum to a more orthodox course on "methodology," and consequently taught by an instructor not conversant with those methods and frequently persuaded that they are merely instinctive fumblings with an ill-defined "data set."

Trained in this way, students must either limit their research to questions appropriate to the few methods they are taught or privately bear the costs of acquiring the methods necessary to do the research they believe needs to be done. Students not engaged in quantitative research—and the faculty they find to guide them—are obliged to bear significantly greater costs in time and labor. Ironically, they, who are obliged to acquire a more extensive methodological education, are required to justify their choices to their more parochial, and less well-trained, colleagues.

65. Formality obscures more than it clarifies.

Formalizations argue, often covertly, but always insistently, that nothing matters as much as the aspect formalized. That must always be interrogated with the questions for what? and for whom? Thus qualified, the contention may be correct, but it is always partial. I might, for example, cast the relation between two prisoners as the Prisoner's Dilemma. In doing so, I would make certain practical imperatives and potential perversities of their relation visible, but whether the prisoner is Antonio Gramsci, Mustafa Dirani, Nelson Mandela, or Charles Manson, much is obscured by the formalization.[117]

66. Every method has an evaluative hierarchy.

Methods carry with them the criteria by which their results are assessed. The form, structures, and procedures of particular methods aim at the fulfillment of certain imperatives and criteria. Structures

---

117. William Sewell, when I first delivered these theses, urged me to change this thesis to the more forgiving "formality obscures as much as it clarifies" or "formality obscures as it clarifies." After some reflection, I have left it as it is. I think it necessary—especially for formalists—to acknowledge that formalizations, seizing as they do on one or two factors or attributes, casting these into high relief and all others into shadow, do indeed obscure more than they clarify and thus require justification. Those like Sewell, who are less tempted by formalism, and so less burdened by its insidious constraints, may be better served by his version of this thesis. Those who have fetishized formalization should have the harsher version thrust upon them.

and procedures require transparency in one's use of sources and procedures, replicability, the display of expertise. These express values of democratic access, both in facilitating assessments of the credibility of the research and researcher, and in enabling (in principle if not in practice) popular testing of the results. They are commonly evangelical, seeking to spread knowledge of the method and its practice through a larger population.

These evaluative criteria are expressive of moral and political values. The theses critical of claims to neutrality, and the accounts given earlier of the formation of identity, recognize that methods, in their conception and practice, cannot escape involvement in politics and systems of morality. Sciences are moralities. Values are entailed in methods.

Some methods have become explicit about the ethical problems entailed in research. This is particularly the case in ethnographic work. Methods disciplining these forms of research often require that people studied know the terms of their involvement in the project and are given the opportunity to critique the finished work of the researcher. These requirements seek to diminish the relation of power between the researcher and those studied and to prevent the researcher from escaping the ethical requirements of the system the researcher entered as a privileged alien. They acknowledge the work of research as exploitative. That these requirements have been neglected in politics and economics, where the alliance of research with war, colonialism, and corporate profit is intricate and enduring, is cause for shame.

67. Every method has an aesthetic.

The aesthetics of method are, not surprisingly, most evident in the methods that protest most vigorously against aesthetics.[118] Consider, for example a presentation in quantitative political science. In

118. This thesis was inspired by a recurrent theme in my conversations with Victoria Hattam, who has recommended the study of contending aesthetics in the discipline of political science.

the early twenty-first century in the United States, such presentations are strictly choreographed performances. They require an overhead projector, a rather cumbersome and antiquated piece of equipment that displays transparencies. Most of these transparencies display "data," or, more precisely, the results of the presenter's quantitative analysis. This is perhaps the most telling aspect of the performance, for the data are commonly nowhere to be seen. The conventions of the presentation oblige the audience to elide the distinction between the data and their quantitative representation, and to assume transparency between these categories. Aesthetics makes arguments.

The transparencies initially displayed in the presentation have a more evidently ritual function. The first transparency gives the title of the talk and, often, the name of the presenter. The second generally displays a list of points to be made during the talk. These are concealed and revealed by means of a sheet of paper which is placed over the list, and gradually moved down as the points are made: an academic dance of the seven veils. In another context, practices of this kind might be seen as indicative of contempt for one's audience, a set of people so obtuse that they are unable to remember the name of the presenter, and require a kind of closed captioning for the learning impaired if they are to grasp the points made in the presentation. Within their genre, these practices are understood as signifiers of professionalism.[119]

Aesthetic considerations govern not only performance but also the collection of information (or data), the designation of appropriate evidence, and the crafting and exposition of arguments. Those who are conscious of themselves as working within language, poststructuralists and hermeneuticists, for example, are given to sophisticated puns and other plays on language. These, which are often multilingual and multidisciplinary in their references, have (appropriately) several effects. They display the speaker's facility with lan-

119. A fuller reading of this, or any other style of presentation, as performance would also examine the preferred sources for metaphors (sports, in the genre cited above) and consider evocations of race, sexuality, class, the permissibility of regionalisms, syntax, and dress.

guage(s) and mastery of multiple disciplines and systems of reference. They foreground the multiple disciplinary and analytic planes
on which the talk will be working, and they signal to the audience
which tropes, metaphors, or words are pivotal in the structure of
the presentation. Plays on language, as this suggests, are not merely
ornamental, nor are they solely displays of expertise. They provide
an economical way of building multiple systems of reference simultaneously. This style of analysis and presentation presumes—and
requires—a competent and attentive audience. Such an audience
will recognize the presence of interconnecting structures and arguments in an analysis that will appear chaotic to those less learned or
unfamiliar with this style.

68. Parsimony is an aesthetic criterion.

Parsimony was once held to be the sine qua non of evaluative criteria in the assessment of theory. At present its value is held, even by
the partisans of science, to be contingent. King, Keohane, and Verba,
still in thrall to the natural sciences, observe that "scholars in physics
seem to find parsimony appropriate, but those in biology often think
of it as absurd." They therefore "do not advise researchers to seek
parsimony as an essential good." They regard parsimony as "a judgement, or even assumption, about the nature of the world: it is assumed to be simple." This reading of parsimony presumes that researchers regard their representations or formalizations of the world
as having a transparent relation of correspondence to that world.
This is not true of mathematics, and I think it unlikely that all partisans of parsimony in the social sciences make that presumption.
The most telling moment in their discussion of parsimony is the remarkable assertion "The clearest definition of parsimony was given
by Jeffreys: 'simple theories have higher prior probabilities.'"[120]
The clarity of this definition is not evident in ordinary language. It

120. King et al., *Designing Social Inquiry*, 20. I would not advise an easy acceptance of their characterization of physics and biology.

is limited to the speakers of a particular highly specialized language, reminding us that clarity, like other evaluative standards, is method-ologically, institutionally, and culturally particular.

King, Keohane, and Verba recognize that taking parsimony as an evaluative criterion entails a broader set of assumptions. They fail to recognize that this evaluative criterion operates on the register of aesthetics. Aesthetic preferences entail both assumptions about the world and hierarchies of values. As an aesthetic criterion, parsi-mony is a form of minimalism, asserting the principle that form should follow function, but, like its counterparts in architecture and design, privileging visual simplicity over simplicity of function. Minimalism, in both fine arts and scholarship, privileged a smooth, unmarked surface, sought a minimum number of planes, required an absence of ornament, and favored textural uniformity. In schol-arship this is expressed through the requirement of linear argument, proscription of references outside the genre. Academic minimalists seek textual as artistic minimalists seek textural uniformity, and both commend the absence of ornament. Limits on the number of arguments (preferably, one) expounded in a given work similarly sought a minimum number of planes in the composition. In both venues, minimalism presents itself as ahistorical and universally ac-cessible. In both venues, it has been followed by a critical return to interiority, historicity, multivocality, and the particular.

69. The form in which something is expressed determines its meaning. The signifier constitutes the meaning of the sign.

Meaning is formed in communities. Different forms of expression speak in different languages to different communities. Translations make many dimensions of meaning accessible across cultures, but the simple phrase "*the scent of jasmine*" does not evoke the same range of historical, literary, or even sensual references as "*le parfum de jasmine*" or "*shum al yasmin*." The effect is more marked in the words "war," "*al-harb*," and "*la guerre*." Even if these words are taken to refer to the same particular war, that war will be understood in relation to the complex of meanings and references in each linguistic, political, and cultural context.

The form that a paper or a document takes tells how that text is to be read. The forms used indicate the other texts it may refer to, appropriate evaluative standards, assumptions, and often specific ambitions and political aims. Forms also give texts different effects. The forms of law are accompanied by the power of the state. The forms monetary value takes—bills or coins or stock certificates— determine how and where they can be used. The expression of Jewish identity through *payes* and *tefillin,* or a Camp Ramah T-shirt, determines the meaning of the identity it constitutes.

This is an observation that, in a slightly different form, bears directly on the work of identity in politics. Derrida's concept of the supplement, one of the many useful and practical tools poststructuralism furnishes, provides an approach to understanding this effect. The supplement, Derrida writes, "adds only to replace."[121] Whether the supplement is the adjectival *woman* or *black* or *Asian,* or the visual apprehension of the signs of race or gender—a shape of hip or eye or nose—it seems to add, and acts to replace. *Woman president* calls up a radically different set of historical and literary references, visual images, imaginary constructs, and evaluative criteria than does *president. Black man* undoes the universality claimed for the category *man,* not simply because it identifies a subset of that category, but because it reveals the racial expectations entailed in *man.*

70. Surfaces are as meaningful as that which lies beneath them.

The meaning of the sign is not contained in the signified alone but in the conjunction of signifier and signified. The race of the French soldier who salutes the tricolor in Barthes's famous example, the representation of Sacagawea with rather than without her child, the

121. Derrida, *Of Grammatology.*

insignia on a uniform, the institution named on the letterhead, the denomination of a piece of currency, are all instances of meaningful differences present on the surface.

Surfaces, moreover, are apt to change their location. The written, though it rests on the surface of a text, contains the depth of the text. In another context, for collectors rather than readers of a text, the composition of ink, paper, leather, and glue may be the site of a text's depths, the vessels that hold the past—and the artifact's genealogy. Dress appears as a superficial matter until one regards dress as a text written on the body, whereupon it reveals itself as holding the depths of an essay on identity. The location of the surface depends upon the angle of examination; superficiality is determined only within a context, in relation to the question at hand. Those who would dismiss the marks of race as surface considerations, observing that consideration of such deeper matters as genetic composition renders them trivial, assume a single plane of meaning. Within the social order, the signs of race may determine access to rights and resources. Signs of religious belief, a beard or circumcision, may be a death warrant.

The error of taking surfaces as meaningless has political and ethical consequences. Similar consequences may arise when researchers or political actors dismiss what they are told, assuming that expressions of loyalty or disavowals of particular opinions are disingenuous.

71. Names constitute. Categories constitute.

Institutions interpellate identities through naming and the creation of categories. Naming and categorization may create rights and rights-bearing individuals, categories may create claims and constituencies.

The choices of the names "pro-choice" and "pro-life" over "anti-abortion" and "pro-abortion" are rhetorical strategies with significant consequences. The question of whether to call the most contentious object of those debates "child" or "fetus" raises issues of legal standing. If it is a child, it is a person, if it is a person it will be ascribed the rights that belong to that name. Similar questions of naming and their consequences accompanied debates over slavery and immigration.

Choosing whether to call the territories in question "the occupied territories," "the West Bank," or "Judea and Samaria" provides an indication of the speaker's position on the status of those territories. Categorizations of Cyprus as Greek or Turkish, Alsace as German or French, were occasions for war.

These strategies can also be found at work in the politics of the academy. One of the more interesting (and revealing) examples is the attempted appropriation of "theory." The authors of *Analytic Narratives* write: "When we refer to theory, we refer to rational choice theory and, most often, to the theory of games. Our advocacy could apply to other forms of theory as well, however."[122] Here Bates and his collaborators attempted the metonymic strategy that Marx identified. They advanced a particular type of theory with the claim that its aims and demands could stand for all. I would argue, however, that this "passage through particularity" has not been "the condition for the emergence of any universalizing effects."[123] On the contrary, the reading of *theory* as a reference solely to "rational choice theory and, most often, the theory of games" was an attempt to constrict the meaning of *theory*. This was necessary in order to sustain the work's claim to novelty. Without a severe constriction of the meaning of *theory*, the extraordinary hubris in the claim to have brought theory to history and history to theory—after Hegel, after Marx, after Weber—would have been too much for the most unblushing partisan.

The title of this work illustrates another effect of naming and categorization. The title (and the announced aim of the enterprise) presupposed the absence of analysis in narrative. *Analytic* was to operate as the Derridean supplement in "analytic narratives," that which adds only to replace. Previous narratives, presumed to be de-

122. Robert Bates, Avner Greif, Margaret Levi, Jean-Laurent Rosenthal, Barry Weingast, *Analytic Narratives* (Princeton, N.J.: Princeton University Press, 1998), 3.
123. Butler et al., *Contingency, Hegemony, Universality*, 45.

void of analysis, were to be replaced by "analytic narratives." Description, however, entails explanation and narrative entails analysis. The effect of the analytic supplement is to disguise the analysis already present in and through the construction of the narrative. Institutionally, the introduction of this category works to diminish the standing of historians and others who employ narrative by deprecating the theoretical content of their work. This suggests the more local and institutional objects of strategic deployments of names and categories in the "analytic narratives" project.

In their appropriation of a narrowed "theory," and in the use of "analytic" as a supplement, Bates and his collaborators illustrated their practical (if unwitting) understanding of illocutionary acts, attempting an institutional restructuring in and as a linguistic one.

72. All categories are subject to an interior articulation and to an articulation of their relations with others. No category is internally homogenous, or independent.

This thesis is a simple reminder that any category can, and often should, be examined for what lies inside and outside it. Finding what lies outside a concept involves the attempt (for these things are not always possible) to give the category a genealogy and identify the conditions of its production. The category can be placed in relation to others. The list in which a given category occurs may change its meaning and practical application. Consider religion in the following lists: astrology, palmistry, tarot, religion; race, sex, nationality, religion. The category of "religion" differs in meaning and function when it appears on an application to parochial school, on a passport, or in an autobiographical essay. "Army" can be seen in relation to such categories as "navy"and "civilian."

The exercise of finding what lies within a concept asks what it is understood to contain and how it is ordered internally. "Army" invites an examination of the structure of command, the relations of officers and men; the hierarchy of values it entails; and the constellation of historical and literary references it evokes. "Religion" can be studied as a system; a system of beliefs, a community bound to—

and by—a particular set of beliefs, practices, and loyalties, a network of institutions. Religion and the army can also be examined through an articulation of their relations with others: labor, capital, the ego, the ideological state apparatus. Each of these efforts gives a more precise understanding of what the use of the category permits and precludes, and what assumptions or ethical positions it may entail.

73. Correlation does not establish causality.

Though it is occasionally neglected in practice, this thesis is widely acknowledged. The most devastating and accurate critique still belongs to Max Weber, who observed that imputing a causal relation on the basis of a correlation was mere "shamanism."[124]

Despite this wide recognition, disciplinary conventions seem to preserve certain aspects of this shamanism. Perform a certain set of rituals properly and (if the gods permit) you will obtain the results. The results may not be what you wish, but they will be informative. If the results are not informative, then it is likely that you have not performed the ritual properly. This should remind us that rigor, like other evaluative criteria, is produced by and in the service of the method it assesses. Scholars from behaviorism to philology and cultural studies continue to be guided by correlations. Such correlations are taken by these late modern shamans as signs. Rather than causing us to dismiss these practices as atavistic, this use of correlations should remind us of its license and limits: the indication of a potential relation.

74. Accurate prediction is not proof of correct reasoning.

Richard Feynman noted that ancient Mayan astronomers were able to furnish far more accurate predictions than those that could be offered by astronomers, or physicists, centuries later. The Mayan cal-

---

124. Weber, *Methodology of the Social Sciences.*

culations, based on observation, were able to predict astronomical phenomena with surprising precision. They were, however, based on wildly errant theories of the universe.[125]

Perhaps it is not surprising that accurate prediction is taken as proof of correct reasoning. Legions of people have, for millennia, predicted the future from the course of the stars, the livers of chickens, the disposition of tea leaves in a cup, or (in the case of a former Canadian prime minister) the whorls of shaving cream and the utterances of a medium. Finding the predictions accurate, they have placed their faith in the processes that produced them: astrology, psychics, tarot, and other methods. If so much of the world, so often and for so long, has taken prediction for proof, why should we expect scholars, even—perhaps especially—scientists, to be exempt?

Furnishing correct predictions is, as Weber recognized, mere shamanism. Though it might, like other forms of shamanism, be useful, it cannot be regarded as a test for theory or an index of correct reasoning. This makes the demand for predictions, occasionally levied in the social sciences as a kind of tax on the exchange of ideas, particularly perverse.

75. Replication is not proof.

This thesis might justly be considered merely a variant of the thesis that correlation does not establish causality. Weber's critique of shamanism applies still more aptly here. The shaman academic performs certain carefully formulated rituals and arrives at the predicted response. Each time the ritual is repeated, the results remain the same. Indeed, the shaman is on firmer ground here, for in many cases, if the shaman performs the ritual correctly, the results will indeed be *exactly* as predicted.

Many years ago I was at a gathering of faculty and graduate students at Princeton University, engaged in a discussion of the various approaches to political science. My then colleague John Zaller ar-

125. I am indebted to the Perestroika listserv for this example from Feynman.

gued vociferously that replicability was a necessary attribute of any work in political science, and he proclaimed proudly (and before witnesses), "Anyone with a Michigan code-book and a high school education can do what I do." Zaller's pride arose from the claim that anyone of mediocre education and abilities could confirm the results of his studies.

This episode interested me first because Zaller's claim did not seem to me to be cause for pride. After some reflection on the occasion for this pride, I realized I found the claim still more interesting. Zaller's pride seemed to come from the method's democratic qualities. The transparency of the method permitted a wide range of people, with limited training and expertise, to evaluate his scholarship and, if they liked, replicate his results.

It is hardly surprising that methods claiming these particular virtues should be particularly prominent (if not preeminent) in the United States. This is a democratic method: accessible to the dull as well as the clever, the ignorant as well as the educated. This is a liberal method: legitimated by a rigorous adherence to procedural rules, privileging the process over the results and valuing transparency. This is a method dependent on convention but insisting that convention receive popular legitimation. If each replication enhances the validity and value of a study, then the most reliable studies will be those that are most easily replicated, by the greatest number of people. The simpler the study, the easier it is to replicate, the more it should be valued.

76. Repetitions alter what they repeat.

There are several senses in which this can be understood.[126] If time is regarded as an attribute of the object studied, then each repetition is, in its temporal aspect, different from those that came before and after. Repetitions, moreover, are always in relation. There is no

---

126. For one more sophisticated than I take up here, see Gilles Deleuze, *Difference and Repetition*, trans. Paul Patton (New York: Columbia University Press, 1994).

simple repetition but a repetition of something. As that thing (or event, or practice) is repeated, it is altered. It may be regarded as the original, and the repetitions consigned to a lower status, or it may be regarded (as in printing) as simply an instance. Even in this latter case, however, repetition alters the repeated, as in a print run where a print may be one of ten, or one of three hundred, and valued accordingly. This is not to suggest that repetition always produces a decrease in value. Under some conventions (as discussed above) repetition may enhance value. This is thought to be the case with citations. Repetition may enhance the influence of a speech, a *hadith*, or a precedent. Those who examine repetition should be attentive to the effect of repetition on value.

Repetition is often important in establishing or communicating meaning. The understanding of an event as a repetition of an earlier one can establish its meaning, with important political consequences. This is also true with regard to political figures whose significance is established by regarding them as a repetition of heroic (or for that matter, nefarious) historical figures. The altering effects of repetition on identities extends from the designation of leaders and epochal figures to the construction and performance of individual identities in everyday life.

77. Falsifiability does not establish validity. Falsifiability is not a necessary attribute of a theory, nor an index of superiority.

Falsifiability is predicated on the notion that the facts, or more precisely, those observations and measurements that are to be considered relevant, must support the theory. Falsifiability demands, moreover, that the theory be supported not by some or most of the facts, but by all of them. This demand has been long discredited in the physical sciences from which its partisans ostensibly take their bearings. As Feyerabend wrote, "No theory ever agrees with all the facts in its domain."[127]

127. Paul Feyerabend, *Against Method* (London: Verso, 1988), 6.

This conception of verification depends upon the assumption that facts exist as such prior to the theories to which they pertain. Facts, however, issue from particular discourses and protocols. They are the creations of theory and technique. Such beings as "the delinquent" and "the criminal" depend upon the prior establishment not only of theories but of institutions, institutional norms, and institutional practices. Facts concerning them operate in relation to these institutions. Once this is recognized, the preoccupation with falsifiability appears as the injunction: no theory may create facts in contradiction to it. This demand runs up against the structure of language and the effects of institutions.

Because of these defects in the concept, falsifiability cannot be considered a necessary attribute of a theory, nor regarded as an index of the superiority of one theory to another.[128]

78. Subjective satisfaction is not an index of the truth or the merit of a theory.

This thesis was written in response to the remarkable contention of Stephen Van Evera that "a good theory is *'satisfying,'* that is, it satisfies our curiosity."[129] This resembles an earlier assessment of validity called "face validity." W. Phillips Shively, who calls this "the most general test of validity," characterized it as "just a fancy term for whether a measure looks right to you."[130]

One might read Van Evera's contention as a play on the discourse of sales, an endorsement of a radical conventionalism. In this reading, Van Evera's claim draws attention to the conventional character of the assessment of truth. Theories are successful when they are accepted. The more people who accept them, the better they are.

128. Contra King et al., *Designing Social Inquiry,* 19, 100–103. Stephen Van Evera, *Guide to Methods for Students of Political Science* (Ithaca: Cornell University Press, 1997), 20.

129. Van Evera, *Guide to Methods,* 19.

130. W. Phillips Shively, *The Craft of Political Research* (Englewood Cliffs, N.J.: Prentice Hall, 1990), 56.

Shively's acknowledgment of this aspect of "face validity" is explicit. If you think the measure "does what you want it to do," he writes, "and people who read your work agree with you," it has "face validity."[131] In this assessment, the reasons for acceptance are irrelevant.

Perhaps the most interesting aspect of this errant contention is the recognition of the imbrication of emotion and intellect in the propagation and internalization of evidentiary standards. Assessments of a theory's worth are in practice, as Van Evera's claim suggests, dependent on emotional as well as intellectual criteria. Van Evera's contention would have been more interesting had he left satisfaction indeterminate, locating validation in the libido, or constructing verification as an instance of intellectual *jouissance*.[132] Unfortunately, Van Evera does not explore these rather interesting avenues.

Van Evera's curious criterion occurs in answer to the question What is a good theory? but it is more importantly linked to an earlier section addressing the question What is a theory? "Theories," he writes, "are general statements that describe and explain the causes or effects of classes of phenomena. They are composed of causal laws or hypotheses, explanations, and antecedent conditions."[133] It is not surprising, given this definition, that Van Evera notes that his instructions on how to write a dissertation apply to all political scientists except those in the field of political theory (which he rather cagily calls "political philosophy").[134] His understanding of theory would apply to few theories recognized as theory by theorists. Perhaps more importantly, this criterion, which presents itself as a limit, operates as a license: exempting those who subscribe to it from the greater demands of theorists.

131. Shively, *The Craft of Political Research,* 56.
132. This would identify the verification of a theory with the "Aha-erlebnis" discussed by Lacan in "The Mirror Stage," *Ecrits.*
133. Van Evera, *Guide to Methods,* 8.
134. Van Evera, *Guide to Methods,* 89, note 1.

79. Systems of knowledge are systems of power.

There is a statement in King, Keohane, and Verba that approaches an acknowledgment of this relation, even as it denies the necessary political consequences. "Science at its best," they write, "is a social enterprise."[135] Science is a social enterprise at its worst and most mediocre as well. Science and all other forms of the pursuit, dissemination, and disciplining of knowledge are conducted within culture. They operate within, and on, social relations. Social capital, educational capital, and financial capital (to borrow Pierre Bourdieu's categories) are all involved in its production. Yet King, Keohane, and Verba, all political scientists, shy away from the recognition that "science is a political enterprise." That recognition came from Pierre Bourdieu, Louis Althusser, Thomas Kuhn, Richard Rorty, and, in its most rigorous and unsparing form, from Michel Foucault.[136]

Foucault's accounts of power/knowledge are the most theoretically rich and precise accounts of the relation of systems of knowledge to systems of power. Writing in "Truth and Power" of the political economy of knowledge, Foucault indicates the extensive integration of political and economic systems of power with systems of knowledge.[137] The "demand for truth" is constantly incited. As the invention, incitement, and diffusion of new needs impels consumption and production, moving a vast economy of circulation and exchange, so the incitement of the demand for truth, the identification of new types of truth to be pursued (the truth about the self, the truth about sexuality, the truth about celebrities) impels the pursuit, production, and dissemination of knowledge. This process of production and dissemination involves the economy of circulation and exchange: producers of knowledge are funded, articles and books

135. King et al., *Designing Social Inquiry,* 9.

136. Bourdieu, *Distinction;* Althusser, "Ideology and the Ideological State Apparatus," in *Lenin and Philosophy.*

137. Michel Foucault, "Truth and Power," in *Power/Knowledge: Selected Interviews and Other Writings 1972–1977,* ed. Colin Gordon (New York: Pantheon, 1980), 131–32.

are circulated and offered for sale, new forms of expertise are available from consultants. This system, like the economic system with which it is intricately involved, is a system of power in its own right; marked by status hierarchies, offering access to resources and influence, enabling coercion; and connected to systems of economic and governmental power. That knowledge produced in universities, in corporate and military research, in the media, is a source of power to be deployed—variously—by the consumers of knowledge: students, scholars, and the public but also the state and particular corporations. The question of the distribution of knowledge, of who will have access to which bodies of knowledge, which pieces of information, which analytic techniques, is contested as a question of power.

There is a rich empirical literature in the social sciences and the humanities on the practical operation of systems of knowledge as systems of power. The complicity of social scientists in the establishment and maintenance of colonial power is one well-explored instance.[138] Certain forms of knowledge (of weaponry, for example) facilitated conquest; knowledge of techniques of domination (Bentham's Panopticon, for example) facilitated governance. Forms of medical, anthropological, linguistic, and other scientific knowledge were deployed in the construction of a colonial subject who would legitimate the colonial rule, in assent or rebellion. Other forms of domination and governance—racial, sexual, and class hierarchies, and the governance of religion—have also deployed these bodies of knowledge. Ironically (perhaps tragically), investigation into the politics of knowledge has become possible only as ethical neutrality has become suspect.

138. Ranajit Guha and Gayatri Chakravorty Spivak, *Selected Subaltern Studies* (New York: Oxford University Press, 1988); Ashis Nandy, *Traditions, Tyrannies and Utopias* (Delhi: Oxford University Press 1987); Timothy Mitchell, *Colonising Egypt* (Cambridge: Cambridge University Press, 1988). In addition to these works, see the politically influential accounts of this process in Sayyid Qutb, *Milestones* (also translated as *Signposts along the Way*), and the more widely available *Islam and Social Justice*.

80. Truth is a cultural category. Truth is in culture.

Truth is occasionally thought to be that at which knowledge aims, outside and above all worldly relations, particularly relations of dominion and subjection. The belief that truth is beyond the reach of power is belied by the relations of power between the learned and the ignorant. The recognition of truths as "compelling" shows how truth operates as power: to compel. Truth may give power or take it away. Truth is worldly: working in and on the world. Truth is a thing of this world: produced and circulated under certain worldly conditions, used and abused in the world, according to worldly norms.

The political conditions governing knowledge altogether hold for truth as well. Foucault writes, "Each society has its regime of truth, its 'general politics of truth': that is, the types of discourse it accepts and makes function as true; the mechanisms and instances which enable one to distinguish true and false statements, the means by which each is sanctioned; the techniques and procedures accorded value in the acquisition of truth; the status of those who are charged with saying what counts as true."[139]

This, which sounds to so many like thorough-going nihilism and an attack on all they hold dear, has familiar manifestations. Consider "the techniques and procedures accorded value in the acquisition of truth" and "the status of those who are charged with saying what counts as true." Institutions like the "newspaper of record"—the *Times* of London, the *New York Times,* or *Le monde*—are charged with saying what counts as true. Quotations or citations of those sources are taken as true. They serve as currency for truth in public discourse. They may be refuted, they may on rarer occasions recant, but they continue to enjoy a privileged position in the regime of truth. Data collections and techniques of measurement function similarly for some in the social sciences. Recently, having queried a particular measurement, I was told by the researcher that while the data was known to be inaccurate, and the measure consequently

139. Foucault, "Truth and Power," in *Power/Knowledge,* 131.

unreliable, there were no better data, use of the defective data was pervasive in her field, and it was accepted as if it were accurate. Both the inaccuracy of the data and the imperative to accept it were confirmed by her colleagues. Popular recognition of this phenomenon is visible in the colloquial phrase "true fact," which recognizes that "fact" and "true" each require supplementary confirmation.

81. Experience confers only a limited understanding.

Like so many of these theses, this is a simple and accessible idea, easily demonstrated in the course of everyday life. I experience electricity on a daily basis. I know how to avoid its most common dangers. I use it. Yet I understand very little about it. If I wished to learn more, I would be better served by reading by candlelight than by electrocution. One might be American and know little of American history; one might vote in Japanese elections without an understanding of the candidates or the electoral system itself. My limited understanding of American politics and history is not primarily the work of experience. It is the result of reading, archival research, classes, symposia, and some thought and conversation on the subject. In order to confer any understanding at all, experience requires reading, research, and reflection. Experience is brief, partial, and particular.

Claims like "I am an American, and I think . . ." or "When I was in Egypt, . . . " make the speaker an artifact, not an authority. The local, individual experience establishes nothing beyond itself (although that may be a great deal). If one generously regards these stories of experience as transparent, one must also recognize that each story can convey no more than the limited experience of a single individual. That experience will be, as all experience is, partial and exceptional.[140]

140. See Joan Scott, "Experience," in *Feminists Theorize the Political,* ed. Judith Butler and Joan Scott (New York: Routledge, 1992).

82. Lies and errors are meaningful.

The first version of this thesis was a recognition I came to in writing my dissertation: if it's not true, it must be important. Whether one works through interviews with the living or among the archives of the dead, one quickly recognizes that people lie and that they are deceived. People are deceived by what they take for granted. People lie in pursuit of ends and desires of some importance to them. Subjects of survey research lie to interviewers because they have second-guessed a survey and wish to influence it in a particular direction. Officials lie to interviewers because they wish to construct their public personae in a particular way, to influence policy, to mislead their opponents, and to control the flow of information. They edit archives to protect their reputations and those of others because they wish to leave a particular portrait of their policies, actions, alliances, enmities, and the reasons for all of these. All subjects may lie out of shame, or pride, the need to protect themselves from hazards or reprisals, or the will to control the manner in which they enter the historical record.

Only a fool would assume that people faced with a survey fill it out in transparent innocence, unconcerned with the survey's object and uninterested in influencing the results. People falsify their answers and intensify their sentiments, knowing that they are offered a small but nevertheless easy and present opportunity for influence. Many are capable (perhaps more capable than the analyst) of seeing what the survey hopes to elicit and of developing strategies for moving the results, however slightly, in the direction they prefer. Surveys taken personally, especially where there is a marked difference (of class or level of education, for example) between the interviewer and the research subject, may be inflected by the subject's reluctance to admit to an inferior status or by the perhaps consequent desire to sabotage the enterprise. Surveys or interviews among recipients of government aid, undocumented workers, or others who could be harmed by the release of information must also account for their probable sense of their own vulnerability.

Only a fool would think that an official, speaking to an interviewer, speaks honestly and transparently. A dedicated and sensible official will always speak with a forked tongue: once in his own interest, and once in the interest of his office. Officials are double subjects, public and private, with obligations to each. This multivocality is complicated by considerations of party and bureaucratic rivalries. The demands of any of these, or conflicts between them, may incline an official to lie. An official—or a citizen for that matter—may have not only an interest in lying but a duty to do so.

The rebellious, the resistant, and the oppressed have reason to lie, to conceal, to deceive. The subaltern acquire a reputation for subtlety or attract the accusation "that they are deceitful, shamming, and lying by nature."[141] Rebels are obliged to conceal their rebellion in order to prosecute it. The poor need to conceal their limited resources and often the means by which they acquired them. The resistant and the oppressed are obliged to conceal their assessments of the legitimacy of the rule over them and their opinions of their rulers. They may reveal these opinions and strategies, but they will do so covertly, and commonly only in the company of their own kind. These strategies are often necessary to the powerful as well. The commanding officer must conceal fear, occasionally ignorance, and often expectations regarding the effects of orders. The colonist must conceal fear, inadequacy, and sentiments ill-suited to the demands of performing imperial authority.

These lies are not, however, immovable obstacles to research. Quite the contrary. The researcher is always confronted with a series of questions and a great indeterminacy. Is the person lying? Is this lie intended for me or for an audience I can reach? Lies, perhaps more than truths, are uttered for reasons. A lie, once discovered, shows that the liar wished to have something else believed and was willing to risk a certain variable degree of shame to that end. Thus while the lie may not provide the evidence it purports to, it does provide evidence of what the liar wished one to believe.

141. Scott, *Domination and the Arts of Resistance*, 3.

Errors can also be evidence. I found when I began to teach that many students would firmly assert that the Allies fought World War II to save the Jews from Hitler. They were not arguing for an understanding of history that made the unconscious Allies bearers of a greater historical mission. They were assuming the motives of the Allies, and they were in error. They were also offering a window onto the reconstruction of the past and evidence (quite invaluable evidence) concerning the meaning of that war for a later generation.

Politics, moreover, is moved not only by the force of reality but by lies and errors. It is the error of taking race for real and not the truth of racial fictions that most often operates in American politics. Errant beliefs about currency and stock values drive both bear and bull markets, impel crashes, and fuel recoveries. Constitutional beliefs that nations stand for "liberty, equality, and fraternity" or that "all men are created equal" in the face of a good deal of empirical evidence to the contrary nevertheless make revolution and reform possible. Lies may act as aspirations and imperatives, requiring states and citizens to overcome themselves.

83. Time is an attribute of the observer, not of the observed.

This simple but still radical thesis comes from Kant. "Time," Kant writes, "is not something which exists of itself, or which inheres in things as an objective determination, and it does not, therefore, remain when abstraction is made of all subjective conditions of its intuition."[142] Time is not an attribute of an outer world free from human perceptions and consequently a source or medium of objective measures. Time is not an attribute or dimension of the physical world. "Time is not an empirical concept that has been derived from any experience."[143]

One might also say with Kant that time is derived *only* from experience: not from that which is experienced but from the manner

142. Kant, *Critique of Pure Reason,* section II, 6a, 76.
143. Kant, *Critique of Pure Reason,* section II, 4.1, 74.

in which we experience it. Time is an attribute of the human, a condition of human understanding, a quality of mind. "Time is nothing but the form of inner sense."[144]

Causality, being dependent on notions of linear time, is not finally defensible. Saying so, however, may prove futile. Wittgenstein writes that "there is nothing more stupid than the chatter about cause and effect in history books: nothing is more wrong-headed, more half-baked.—But what hope could anyone have of putting a stop to it just by *saying* that?"[145] This thesis shares Wittgenstein's (and Kant's) apparently futile aim. Having, however, lower ambitions, less shame, and perhaps more practicality, two other courses will be proposed here. The first (and more honorable) will be taken up in thesis 85, where I offer a different way of thinking of causality. The second, more expedient course is proposed here:

Many may find causality useful as an analytic convention, metaphor, or hermeneutic device. If this convenient, but misleading and compromised, course is adopted, the following theses, otherwise superseded, become relevant:

83a. Causality is reciprocal.

This subordinate thesis can be considered as a corrective to the simple linearity characteristic of causal arguments. Those relations that appear to be most asymmetrical nevertheless show mutual influence. For a fuller, more detailed example, consider the Raj. The relation of dominion and subjection in which imperial Britain held India during the period of colonial rule did not preclude Indian influences on the British. The British learned not only to play polo, to eat kedgeree and curry, and to have their princes and their officers wear turbans and jodphurs. They also learned strategies and practices of governance, principles of philosophy and spiritual inquiry, narrative forms, and mathematical propositions.

144. Kant, *Critique of Pure Reason*, section II, 6.b, 77.
145. Wittgenstein, *Culture and Value*, 62e.

This subordinate thesis might also be considered as a simple technique. When one identifies a direction of influence, one should always turn it around. When one identifies an influence, one should look for it to work in reverse. Presidents influence parties, parties influence presidents. Criminality prompts legislation, policing, and study; legislation, policing, and study interpellate criminality.

Identifying reciprocal causality steadily undermines linear causality, for each moment of influence has an attendant reciprocal effect. As effect becomes cause, and cause effect, the line of causality becomes a network in which relations are formed.

83b. There are always multiple causes.

Children discover one variant of this thesis early on when they learn to ask Why? Each cause must have a cause of its own. As they inquire further, a simple relation of cause and effect becomes a chain of causality. Even in this all-too-linear scheme, causes multiply. The effect may be traced back to an Executive Order, and further to vigorous lobbying of a President. Both of these can be put forward as causes of the Order, and each will have other causes behind it.

Another variant is discovered almost as early. If one asks What was the cause of the al Aqsa Intifada? one can answer: Ariel Sharon's visit to the Temple Mount, Yasser Arafat's encouragement of a violent response, continuing incitement to war, the Oslo accords, the failure of the Oslo accords, or the proliferation of settlements in the occupied territories. With this, as with most examples from politics, multiple causes indicate multiple explanations. The diversity of causes reflects not only diverse explanations but also the diverse aims and evaluations inherent in those explanations and the diverse positions from which they come.

Multiple causes are not, however, simply the work of ideological difference, or even differences in perspective. They are also a consequence of the complex networks structuring events. In the political world, nothing happens in isolation. That which happens within language, within culture, within politics, happens within a network of meaning. The connections that link people and events in that network ensure that any event will have not one but multiple causes.

84. A statement of a causal relation is not a theory. Theory does not require causality.

As Weber observed, postulating a cause-and-effect relation may be no more than mere shamanism. The definition of theory as simply a statement of a causal relation is a niggardly and undemanding definition at best. It lacks the demand for an explanation. Postulating a cause-and-effect relation is not enough: theory requires that such claims be accompanied by an account of the mechanics. When Socrates makes the remarkable claim that we never discover, we only remember, he provides through a slave a demonstration of the mechanics of remembering. When Marx gives a theory of history, he provides an account of the engine that moves history forward and of where, how, and on what that engine works. One must know *how* the putative cause produces the ostensible effect.

Given this shortcoming, it is not surprising that theorists dismiss the definitions of theory prevailing in the methodological literature or that methodological literature makes stringent efforts to steer clear of theorists. What is surprising is that this slacker's stand-in for theory is advanced as a criterion for rigor.

To regard the positing of a cause-and-effect relation as essential to theory is to make a word in common use, with a long history, into a parochial neologism. According to King, Keohane, and Verba; Bates; Shively; and Van Evera, there is little or nothing in Plato, Montaigne, Montesquieu, Rousseau, or Nietzsche that could be regarded as a theory. The older, more common, use of the word *theory,* separated from the jargon of a particular school, admitted many forms of inquiry under that rubric. Theories were not required to postulate cause-and-effect relations (although, if they did, they were required to do considerably more). Theories also revealed paradoxes, delineated complex patterns of relationship, envisaged forms of life, offered ethical guidance, and raised perhaps insoluble questions. This more generous understanding of theory, refined by time and common use, does not exclude the fields of politics and ethics. Instead, it opens the possibility that the scholar might offer not only something to knowledge but something to life.

85. Schemes of causality are narrative fictions driven by illusory personifications.

"The insidious thing about the causal point of view," Wittgenstein writes, "is that it leads us to say 'Of course it had to happen like that.' Whereas we ought to think: it may have happened like *that*— and also in many other ways."[146] Many of those who make causal arguments aim explicitly at furnishing the definitive account, the sole answer, the only explanation. Wittgenstein is a step ahead of these. Knowing this explanatory finality to be impossible, he nevertheless recognizes how the causal point of view offers the allure of a singular explanation. If one is to retain the uses of causal explanations without falling prey to false claims of closure, one must come to think of causal schemes in a different manner, one that makes more modest and more accurate claims and requires more rigorous proofs for closure. That is what this thesis proposes.

A causal scheme is a story. Like other classic narratives it has generic forms, and like all stories, it has characters. These narratives, these stories of cause and effect, classically concern such characters as "France" and "Germany" or "the proletariat" and "the Church." They may also be peopled with such figures as "the market," "the state," "institutions," and occasionally "discourses" who occupy roles elsewhere described as those of the dependent and independent variables. These figures have motives, intention, and agency. There are disputes about their relations to each other, their "relative autonomy," for example, or "interdependence." The personifica-

146. Wittgenstein, *Culture and Value*, 37e.

tions that people the narrative are illusory and anthropomorphic, ascribed not only intentions and actions but also moods, dispositions, and moral character.

These personifications, "the state" and "the market," for example, are embedded in a narrative that tells a story about that relation. The narrative is a fiction. Freud, in writing of the murder of the primal father and the subsequent totemfeast, described it, with characteristic honesty, as "a just-so story."[147] The same might be said of the various myths of social contract so prominent in the Western canon, Rawls's "original position," or the Prisoner's Dilemma.

Rational choice and game theory are perhaps the richest depositories of stories, in the most traditional sense, offering us not only the Prisoner's Dilemma but also the Battle of the Sexes, Burning Money, the Grim Trigger, and the Chain Store Paradox. These have plot, characters, motive, atmosphere. As James Morrow noted, "The Battle of the Sexes has a cute slice of life in the 1950s built into its story" in which a husband and wife debate whether to go to a prize fight or the ballet.[148] Chicken belongs to the same period.

> Back in the 1950s, teenaged males suffering from excessive hormones would engage in a contest of manhood known as Chicken. The two contestants would meet on a deserted stretch of road, each driving their favorite machine. They would face each other at some distance and drive their cars directly at each other until one driver "chickened" out by swerving off the road. The other would be the winner and would be proclaimed the man with the most hormones on the block. Sometimes neither driver would chicken out, and many hormones would be spilled on the pavement.[149]

147. Sigmund Freud, *Totem and Taboo*.
148. James Morrow, *Game Theory for Political Scientists* (Princeton, N.J.: Princeton University Press 1994), 91.
149. Morrow, *Game Theory for Political Scientists*, 93.

Most of the games Morrow describes are accompanied by what he calls "a cute story." These stories derive variously from literature (Thomas Schelling uses Melville's Ahab as a protagonist), history (the Cuban missile crisis), and popular culture. They tend to be simple in structure, although like Julio Cortazar's *Hopscotch*, each has not one but several possible narrative structures within it. The prisoner may cooperate or defect, the couple may go to the prizefight or the ballet. They tend to rely on—and they require the transmission of—conservative conceptions of social roles, though this may be deprecated, as in Morrow, by the narrator's adoption of an ironic tone. In short, these games, like other stories, transmit more than formal models of strategic situations.

Historical narratives, as Hayden White observed, also have distinctive rhetorical characteristics. "For example, in Michelet the idiographic form of explanation is coupled with the plot structure of the Romance; in Ranke the organicist explanation is coupled with the comic plot structure; in Tocqueville the mechanistic mode of explanation is used to complement and illuminate an essentially Tragic conception of the historical process; and in Burckhardt a contextualist explanatory mode appears in conjunction with a narrative form that is essentially satirical."[150] In this work, White demonstrates how the tools of rhetoric and literary criticism can be employed to analyze the narrative structures of historical work. He reminds us too that the recognition of history as a work involving the imagination is not a novel one.[151]

Political—and other social—scientists too often labor under the assumption that narrativity belongs to history, and that narrativity appears in the social sciences only where they are under the influence of historical methods. They labor under a misapprehension. All causal explanations are historical. They depend upon (as they advance) a linear conception of history. Within each explanation is

150. Hayden White, *Tropics of Discourse* (Baltimore: Johns Hopkins University Press, 1978), 66.
151. White, *Tropics of Discourse*, 83–84.

a temporal scheme: the cause comes before the effect. The explanation offers a simple, parsimonious history of the effect in question. The minimalist aesthetic operative in these brief historical narratives does not strip them of other rhetorical attributes.

This value of this thesis lies not in the debunking of their truth-claims to those still wedded to the fictions of scientific discovery and value-neutral facts but in pointing toward a set of analytic tools and marking sites for their use. The recognition that causal explanations are narratives indicates the value of the tools of rhetorical analysis and other forms of literary criticism. Recognition of the narrativity of modes of social scientific enquiry opens up new terrain for methodological analysis and critique.

86. Culture has dimensions in time and space.

Culture is material and has dimensions in time and space. Cultures and the cultural exist in particular places at particular times. They occupy territorial spaces (though these are not always contiguous, or coincident with political entities). They have boundaries in time. One must look for the physical site of a culture, its spatial form and dimensions, and its place in time, its historical moment. This is a simple but important principle for research into politics and culture. I mean, however, for the thesis to go further.

Whether one looks to culture as the particular form of being in language, or sees culture in and as the objects, people, and events who are its products and producers, culture is physically present. Culture operates through this physicality. The regulations of food and sex and dress that accompany the world's great religions acknowledge and exploit the physical: the senses of touch and smell and taste, the effects of habit on movement, of custom on taste. One does not need to read Deuteronomy or Leviticus, however, to know cultures through the senses. Sensation can also enable us to experience, in the most intimate and evocative way, the hinge between the temporal and spatial dimensions of culture. For me, the scent of jasmine, or durian, or other scents for which I have no name calls up Bangkok in the time of the war in Vietnam. Eating sticky rice and *lad na,* drinking thick, sweet coffee, touching silk, or moving in a low boat through water belonged to that time and place and remain as its remnants, signs, and evocations. People experience their cultures physically: in what they wear and how they wear it, what they eat, what they smell, what they see, what they hear, and how and when and at what speed they move. Work on culture, and on politics in culture, is not restricted to the study of books and documents but extends to all those sites in which culture has physical presence.

For those who study politics, culture's presence in material forms is particularly evident in the study of race, ethnicity, sexuality, and violence. The body is not only a text on culture but also the site of culture's incarnation and enactment, of political performances and constitution. Architecture and territoriality, boundaries and trade flows, give culture dimensions in time and space. These dimensions inform the work of scholars throughout the social sciences, even those most reluctant to acknowledge the importance of cultural inquiry.

87. Cultures have tempi.

Weber wrote that industrial development reached so thoroughly into culture and altered people so profoundly that "it changed their natural rhythms."[152] Giorgio Agamben writes, "Every conception of history is invariably accompanied by a certain experience of time which is implicit in it, conditions it, and thereby has to be elucidated."[153] Like Weber, Agamben believes that modernity's tempo echoed rhythms of industrial manufacture. Both recognized that changes in material conditions, in this case, in the conditions of labor,

152. Weber, *From Max Weber,* trans. and ed. H. H. Gerth and C. Wright Mills (New York: Oxford University Press, 1946), 261.
153. Giorgio Agamben, "Time and History" in *Infancy and History: Essays on the Destruction of Experience,* trans. Liz Heron (New York: Verso, 1993), 91.

could alter—had altered—the experience of time. Workers ate and slept, entered and left, according to the factory bell or the timeclock. During the day, they moved their bodies according to the inalterable imperatives of the machines with which they worked. As the model of the factory (or perhaps it is the church or the army) spread to the school, the clinic, the prison, and the asylum, children and teachers, patients and doctors, the mad, the criminal, and their caretakers fell into the rhythms of the factory.

It is a commonplace that cities and rural areas, modernity and tradition, enclose lives lived at different speeds. Farmers observe the rhythms of the natural world, the change of seasons, the growth of crops and animals, the cycles of laying and milking. When they alter these, particularly with the mechanization of agriculture, they move into another lifeworld. Tradition is often said to move more slowly than modernity. Koselleck writes of "the peculiar acceleration which characterizes modernity," and Virilio marked speed as modernity's distinguishing attribute. [154]

For Benjamin and Deleuze, among others, it is repetition that characterizes modernity: a steady, uniform rhythm. These rhythms are audible in the regular, repetitive sounds of machinery. They are visible in mechanical reproduction: the repeated images made possible by printing, lithography, photography. They are productive in mass manufacture. Factory work, and the disciplines of church and school, inculcate repetitive rhythms.[155]

These diverse recognitions of the importance of rate and rhythm in cultures demonstrate that taking time as a plane of analysis entails more than asking When? or For how long? Questions of chronology and duration begin the enquiry; they do not end it. Working

---

154. Reinhardt Koselleck, *Futures Past: On the Semantics of Historical Time,* trans. Keith Tribe (Cambridge, Mass.: MIT Press, 1985), 5. Paul Virilio, *Speed and Politics,* trans. Mark Polizzotti (New York: Semiotexte, 1986).

155. Walter Benjamin, "The Work of Art in the Age of Mechanical Reproduction," in *Illuminations,* trans. Harry Zohn, ed. Hannah Arendt (New York: Schocken Books, 1968), 217–52. Gilles Deleuze, *Difference and Repetition;* Foucault, *Discipline and Punish.*

on the plane of time also involves asking questions about rate, rhythm, and repetition: How fast? How frequently? What is repeated? In what cycle? In what pattern? Who can keep up? Who falls behind? What is the tempo of the Sorrow Songs?

88. If one can ask where, then one can also ask when. If one can ask when, one can ask where.

This is one of the theses I mean to be useful and practical, and I mean it very literally. If one can ask When is the United States founded? one can, one should, one must, ask Where is the United States founded? If one can ask Where are the Palestinians? one can, one should, one must, ask When are the Palestinians? This tool becomes most useful when the questions it prompts seem most awkward.

I have gone out on a limb a bit with this thesis, since I am not prepared to say why it is the case that one can ask where when one asks when, or when where one asks where. I think the best suggestions occur in Heidegger's essay "Building Dwelling Thinking," in which he discusses the relation of time (the time of the interval) to space and the interval as a space in which thought emerges. A simpler, if ultimately less satisfying, explanation might be that this thesis reminds one that any event has both a temporal and spatial location, and that it is necessary to know both in order to locate the event correctly. This protocol follows the old principles of celestial navigation.

89. What comes before may have come after.

A condition or event can come into being as a precondition during or after the emergence of that for which it becomes the precondition.

This observation would seem to offer a rather serious affront to linear conceptions of time and history, yet it is widely relied upon, and examples of its use are common.

Those who take the social contract to be something other than a

historical event in the ordinary sense cast the state of nature as exactly that: a precondition preceding that for which it is the precondition, made a precondition by what follows it. The state of nature
does not simply exist prior to contract as the justification for contract, it comes into being as such only after the political begins. In
those systems that see morality as conventional rather than as a form
of natural law, the moral imperatives that justify the social contract
emerge only after morality is established in convention. Language
gives us many things as prior to language: nature, culture, the speaking and writing body.

The same logic informs Charles Tilly's characterization of the
war-making state as a protection racket. Tilly observes that the state
promises to protect one from a threat that does not exist apart from
the protection the state provides.[156] The state, operating as *capo di
tutti capi,* creates the very threat it provides protection from. Recognition of this effect thus undermines the state's legitimacy insofar as
it is based on these guarantees of peace and order. Tilly's essay under-
lines the pervasiveness of this seemingly counterintuitive phenomenon. As he argues, the logic of state-making depends upon taking an
effect for a precondition. This seemingly perverse logic is pervasive
not only in theories of contract but also in the broader logic justifying the war-making state. Tilly brings the ethical implications of this
thesis to the fore.

For Locke, not only wrongs suffered but wrongs anticipated warrant punishment. One might kill a thief, Locke wrote in a famous
passage, "who has not in the least hurt him, nor declared any design upon his Life . . . because using force where he has no Right, to
get me into his Power, let his pretence be what it will, I have no reason to suppose, that he, who would take away my Liberty would
not when he had me in his Power, take away every thing else.[157]

---

156. Charles Tilly, "War-making and State-making as Organized Crime" in
Bringing the State Back In, ed. Peter Evans, Dietrich Rueschmeyer, Theda
Skocpol (Cambridge: Cambridge University Press, 1985).

157. John Locke, *Second Treatise,* sec. 18, in *Two Treatises of Government,*
ed. Peter Laslett (Cambridge: Cambridge University Press, 1963).

In this accounting, a privileged sign of imminent threat becomes currency for the harm it is said to threaten. The right to kill the thief derives from an act that has yet to happen, a harm that has yet to occur, a debt that has yet to be contracted. The one who will kill (but would not have) confronts a thief who will not kill (but might have). In this theft, the calculus of responsibility serves to incite the violence it pretends to prevent. Because the calculation of responsibility is dependent on a clear chain of cause and effect, recognizing that the chain is reversed in this instance undermines not only Locke's ethical claims but all claims dependent on the same form.

This thesis should open the door to two critiques: a critique of conventional understandings of causality, and an attendant critique of the ethic of responsibility, which depends upon a linear understanding of cause and effect.

90. The past is accessible only in and as the present.

The simplest and most readily accepted reading for this thesis is one that carries the reminder that the past, in its wholeness, is closed to us. We cannot return to the past, or enter a past not our own, except in very partial and limited ways. We can hold objects from the past. We can read documents from the past. We can bind objects from the past together in an imagined recollection of the past. All of the things we use to make imaginary reconstructions of the past come to us in the present, as parts of the present. This is true of us as well. Insofar as we come to the past, we come to it from the present, and as a people of the present. We enter the past in the same way we enter Disneyland's Main Street, or Colonial Williamsburg. We enter those places through gates and parking lots that mark them as reconstructions. We enter in contemporary clothing, bringing with us contemporary discourses, contemporary mores, contemporary norms. We recognize our reconstructions of the past as reconstructions, whether we enter them through the Disneyland parking lot or through research. We do not expect, when we open an archived document or enter a reconstruction of an era that we will find ourselves in the past.

In taking this position I set myself against those who argue that an artifact of the past, an object that has survived from the past contains the past within it.[158] The material object, once present in the past, now present for us, brings the past to us. The past is not, however, something that might be carried in (or as) a vessel. Past and present cultural moments meet in material objects that, made in the past, may be held in the present. This is commonly recognized. People who regard their land as linking them to ancestors who also lived upon it work from that understanding. Traditions of historic preservation and traditions of pilgrimage both use the materiality of culture as a link between present and past. Neither Benjamin's arguments nor these practices, however, argue that one can leave the present for the past. Rather, they acknowledge the materiality of culture and observe the effects (and uses) of that materiality.[159] Insofar as the past comes to us as and in it, the past comes to us as and in the present.

The conviction that artifacts, material objects, may hold the past within them does suggest a startling and potentially fecund thesis: the past is accessible to us through the senses. The past is said to be inaccessible because people die, practices alter, cities, buildings, and monuments decay, records are lost. The loss of the past is ascribed to its materiality, which denies it the capacity for endurance. Yet it is in the material that the past endures. It is through the senses that one gains access to the past.

I put this thesis (and its more subversive companion) forward somewhat tentatively. The dichotomy of past and present that the

158. Walter Benjamin, "The Work of Art in the Age of Mechanical Reproduction," in *Illuminations*. This essay contains important and influential discussions of authenticity and the relation of mechanical reproduction to mass culture. This is one of the important sites at which politics and aesthetics meet.

159. This echoes Michael Oakeshott's recognition that an artifact testifies only to itself. *Experience and Its Modes* (Cambridge: Cambridge University Press, 1995).

thesis presents is a misleading one, and although it seeks to undermine the dichotomy, the repetition of these terms may have the effect of reifying it instead. The categories "past," "present," and "future" have the feel of well-worn tools. They have served well, and in a skilled hand they are not too rough for fine work. Here I can only attach the reminder that these are all categories that belong to us, which describe a sense of time that belongs to us and not to a world apart from us. The thought that the past is present to us, materially, sensually, may suggest avenues of enquiry that will continue to undermine the pervasive, and pervasively misleading, understandings of the relation of past and present.

91. The designation of origins is a political act.

This simple thesis is readily illustrated empirically. In the antebellum United States, there were those who argued for a Puritan founding, locating the origin of the nation at Plymouth Rock, on the occasion of the Pilgrim's landing. This account of the nation's origins made the founders Puritans, and placed the Constitution in a lineage of covenants that reached through the Mayflower Covenant to the covenants of the New and Old Testament. The political effects of this designation were manifold and profound. The Constitution privileged the northern states. It legitimated efforts to exclude, disenfranchise, or assimilate large numbers of recent Catholic immigrants. Those who placed the site of the nation's origins in Philadelphia in 1776 contended for a more secular and revolutionary founding. This designation could be (and was) used to legitimate a southern secession that was said to reenact the colonial states' Declaration of Independence from British rule. Those who have argued that we must see the United States as a Christian nation, govern it in accordance with Christian tenets, and privilege Christian institutions have also relied on the Puritan founding to legitimate religious activism and intervention in public life.

Such debates are by no means peculiar to the United States. They are conducted with great openness and vigor in India, where debates over the designation of origins have extended to public debates over scholarly works in history and archaeology. These debates extend into popular culture as well. A series of comic books on Indian history provides its own history of the nation's origins, prefacing each comic book with a justification of the position of the series.[160] Egypt is riven—and invigorated—by debates that set a Pharaonic against a Muslim past.

As this suggests, any scholarly work that involves the designation of origins will have political effects and must be understood as a political act. There is no neutrality here. In most cases, particularly the most hazardous and contentious cases, the question When does it begin? entails the question What is it?

92. There is no incorruptible discourse. There is no perfect method.

The search for methods, and for rigor in methods, is impelled by the desire to escape one's own fallibility. This is the promise of liturgy, sacrament, and ritual for a secular priesthood: if you adhere to the ritual, if you follow the liturgy, grace will come. This is the promise of the machine: if you make a machine to do something properly it will do that thing properly until it breaks down. No ritual works in all circumstances; no machine can accomplish all tasks. Sacraments bring grace to and through those already graced. Machines create new processes and products, and with them new accidents, defects, and injuries.

Some have thought this difficulty can be resolved by seeking a social science that "solves problems." They forget that when this has been done, the results have not been entirely satisfactory. The development of the prison system was an effort at solving the problem of inhumanity in discipline, surveillance, punishment, and reform. The colonial project enlisted generations of scholars in solving problems: problems of penetration, problems of domination, problems of

160. *Rani of Jhansi* (Bombay: Amar Chitra Katha, n.d.).

rebellion. The Cold War, Vietnam, and liberal economics have all been efforts at solving problems. A commitment to solving problems is no panacea.

The search for a pure discourse, the effort to reform language, to seek clarity and precision in speech and writing is impelled by the desire to make communication ever more open and universal, to make meaning stable over time. These are efforts contrary to language. Languages are made, and change, in practice, and so their future meaning cannot be foreseen. Acts of writing have effects beyond the intention of their authors, and those effects cannot be predicted or controlled. Meanings are made, and strategies must operate, in contexts. Contexts change.

The pursuit of a purer language may also be impelled by political desires or offer an elusive political promise. The discourse of rights, which promised so much to so many, argued for the freedom of the slave but it also argued for the property of the slaveholder; for the rights of women, but also for the rights of the unborn and the rights of the husband within his household. There is no discourse immune to appropriation, and none that remains under the authority of its ostensible authors.

The hope for a tool that will not turn in the hand, for a language that will speak without deception, for a method that cannot be used irresponsibly, is illusory.

93. The ideal appears in the material.

This thesis has a distinguished ancestry, but here it serves only the very limited task of reminding readers that theories, ideas, values, concepts, and norms take material form. They have presence, they are worldly. They are visible, audible, legible.[161] They can be

---

161. This thesis and the one that follows might be called "simple things one learns from Hegel." While it is only right to acknowledge my debt to Hegel and to direct others to that work, I am reluctant to involve myself or an unsuspecting reader in the elaborate disputes that cluster around the relation of the material to the ideal in the philosophic literature on Hegel.

tasted, smelled, touched. There is no object, no thing, that does not give ideas to us in and through its sensible, material form. Whether one believes that rocks call to the geologist, or call forth the geologist, or that the geologist calls rocks into being, one sees the operation of an imperative to open, to investigate, in relation to material things. Set that aside, and look to politics. One can take the nation as an idea, and its forms as mere expressions of that idea, but when one looks to those forms—to land, law, and nationals—the reduction of these to mere expressions becomes untenable. One can take land, and look to territories and boundaries, to the conditions, products, and boundaries of the land, or to the myriad traits and actions of citizens and nationals, and find that these do not, despite their own inexhaustibility, account for the nation. One might look at the ideal as the surplus value of the material, as its excess or perhaps as the productive effect of the inadequacy of the material.

The ideal, the theoretical, is always present in empirical work. Matter is a form of revelation.

94. The abstract appears in the particular.

As the ideal appears in the material, the abstract likewise appears in that which is most individual, most singular, most particular. Though abstraction might be thought to belong to generality, it is found (in generous multiplicity) in the small particularities of the world: in human beings certainly, but in simple objects as well. It is through material objects that we come to know one, red, hard, wet, round, cold, seeing, and hunger. It is through play with these objects that one comes to know likeness and difference; inside, over, and after; presence and absence.

The particular is not an illustration of one abstraction alone nor a simple, unaccompanied instance of that abstraction.

In light of this, the idea that abstract work is more demanding or superior in sophistication is an instance not merely of unmerited arrogance but of a rather startling ignorance. The problem with particularity, for those of us who deal in abstractions, is not that it is too simple but that it is too complex. Abstractions permit us to bring the particular within our limits.

95. Theory cannot exhaust the particular.

The ideal and the abstract make not one but many appearances in any particular object or instance. These—these people, this person, this date, this hour, this nation, this house, this hand, this document, this letter—are not carriers of a single idea or manifestations of a small complex of abstractions. No theory can exhaust the materiality, the signifying capacity, the ideality, of the particular. Each instance, each thing, is a gate into the infinite.

Afterword

These 95 theses were not, like their namesakes, nailed to a church door. They were presented at a meeting of the American Political Science Association. Like their namesakes, they were directed against an orthodoxy. They spoke to a hierarchy that is, if not corrupt, certainly at odds with its professed values and with the better practices of its clergy and laity. This commentary on the theses continues dissent from, and a challenge to, that hierarchy and that orthodoxy. They are addressed not to the methodological authorities in the discipline of political science but to the students who have chosen better ways to work on politics. I hope that they are of interest beyond these boundaries.

Wittgenstein makes two observations that I attach here like a *mezuzah,* to identify my loyalties, to acknowledge a better, and to ward off evil. He writes, "If someone is merely ahead his time, it will catch him up one day."[1] Nothing here is ahead of its time; everything is following after practice. These theses attempt to capture, in simple terms, how many thoughtful scholars think of work on politics, culture, and method. These have become so well integrated into our practices, so taken for granted as theoretical governance, that it is sometimes difficult to recover the textual sites where they are made explicit and the arguments that support them. My formulations in the first 95 theses, and in the commentary I have, with the help of many others, furnished on them here, are often crude. The citations are inadequate. I can assure you, however, that where I have erred, it is in the direction of insufficient radicalism. The finest

1. Ludwig Wittgenstein, *Culture and Value,* trans. Peter Winch, ed. G. H. von Wright (Chicago: University of Chicago Press, 1980), 8e.

work in the field is disciplined by guiding principles more rigorous, more refined, and more radical than these.

Catching up with practice has not always been easy for me, but I had help. Jim Scott suggested I expand the original 95 theses into this longer form and encouraged Yale to publish it. John Kulka, my editor; Jim Morone; and an anonymous reader offered incisive, amusing, and altogether brilliant suggestions for revision. Joyce Ippolito, dealing gracefully with an eccentric manuscript, did as well. Where I followed them (which is rather often) the text is better for it. Michael Rogin had the manuscript when he died. The silence where his comments should be reminds me of a greater silence. The work this book fed on owes much to him. William Sewell, Jeffrey Tulis, and Lisa Wedeen provided invaluable comments on the original theses, which I have tried to incorporate. Victoria Hattam suggested the panel, worked with me on it, and read this longer text. Uday Mehta dared me to think of 95 theses in the first place. The theses on identity were discussed and critiqued at a seminar at the New School for Social Research organized by Victoria Hattam and Ernesto Laclau. I am especially obliged to Yannis Stavrakakis for his comments there. I am also indebted to scholars I first knew as graduate students and now happily have as colleagues, particularly Alev Cinar, Srirupa Roy, Joe Glicksberg, Joe Mink, Kevin Bruyneel, Joe Lowndes, Tamara Waggener, Jim Henson, Wambui Mwangi, and Vikash Yadav. Jeff Tulis gave an early draft to his class on methods. I am obliged to these people for their reading and their suggestions. Perestroika and the Perestroika list, and the Ethnohistory Seminar at the University of Pennsylvania, provided examples and were examples in themselves. The Alfred L. Cass term chair provided support. I have gotten warnings, ideas, and inspiration from Deborah Harrold, Bob Vitalis, Maggie Browning, Tom Dumm, Ellen Kennedy, and Rogers Smith. I did not always listen to their warnings, but I have always learned from their work.

Throughout the work, I set myself against certain works and scholars. I have chosen these carefully. I had no wish to damage the career of a promising scholar. I believe, moreover, that one often learns most from one's opponents. Consequently, I have chosen to critique only scholars with established reputations—reputations that I believe to be deserved. I've learned a great deal from them and although some may find it odd, I expect they will understand and appreciate this rather perverse tribute.

Wittgenstein writes that for him, his way of thinking is new: "That is why I need to repeat myself so often. It will have become second nature to a new generation, to whom the repetitions will be boring. I find them necessary." For me, many of these ideas are new. Even those to which I have become accustomed are not yet second nature. Repetition for me is a form of training and self-discipline, a regimen. Soon I hope it will be, as it is for others, child's play.